The Band Teacher's Percussion Guide

The Band Teacher's Percussion Guide

Insights into Playing and Teaching Percussion

Stewart Hoffman

OXFORD
UNIVERSITY PRESS

Oxford University Press is a department of the University of Oxford. It furthers
the University's objective of excellence in research, scholarship, and education
by publishing worldwide. Oxford is a registered trade mark of Oxford University
Press in the UK and certain other countries.

Published in the United States of America by Oxford University Press
198 Madison Avenue, New York, NY 10016, United States of America.

Library of Congress Cataloging-in-Publication Data
Names: Hoffman, Stewart, author.
Title: The band teacher's percussion guide : insights into playing and teaching
percussion / Stewart Hoffman.
Description: New York : Oxford University Press, [2017] |
Includes bibliographical references and index.
Identifiers: LCCN 2016022325 (print) | LCCN 2016023436 (ebook) |
ISBN 9780190461683 (cloth : alk. paper) | ISBN 9780190461690 (pbk. : alk. paper) |
ISBN 9780190461706 (updf) | ISBN 9780190461713 (epub)
Subjects: LCSH: Percussion instruments—Instruction and study. |
Education, Secondary.
Classification: LCC MT655 .H62 2017 (print) | LCC MT655 (ebook) | DDC
786.8/193071—dc23
LC record available at https://lccn.loc.gov/2016022325

9 8 7 6 5 4 3 2 1

Paperback printed by WebCom, Inc., Canada
Hardback printed by Bridgeport National Bindery, Inc., United States of America

Dedicated to the memory of my teacher, Elden C. "Buster" Bailey.
A giant among percussionists, and a beautiful human being.

CONTENTS

ACKNOWLEDGMENTS

I am greatly indebted to a number of people who have contributed in so many different ways toward the development of this book.

To Morris "Arnie" Lang, whose encouragement, support, and input are valued so very much, a heartfelt thank you.

To David Friedman, a profound musical presence in my life and a source of inspiration since my first vibraphone lesson, thank you for your encouragement and helpful suggestions.

I am greatly indebted to Paul McLaughlin, my writing teacher, who has provided so much support for this project and all my writing endeavors.

Thank you to Maggie Thompson for your perspective, input, and encouragement early on, as well as to Lee Willingham and Rob Waring for providing early feedback.

Many thanks to Lorne Nehring, Ray Dillard, and Adam David for so generously sharing your expertise, as well as to Stefan Bauer, Beverly Johnston, Russell Hartenberger, and Bill Cahn for the helpful conversations and emails.

I am deeply saddened that my friend Robin Engelman, who passed away a few short weeks after advising me on chapters of this book, is unable to join with me in the celebration of its publication. I did not know at the time how much that last afternoon together at his home would mean to me.

Thanks to the administration and staff at Crescent School for so generously providing access to the instruments and space for photography, and to the music teachers—Vince Volpe, Brian Crone, and Harry Timmermans—for fielding any and all annoying questions I may have presented to you.

Thank you to Chris Reesor and Yamaha Canada, Barbara Freedman, Jon Rosenberg, Jack Gelbloom, Stan Pearl, Paul Emond, Eleanor Engelman, Martin Loomer, and Michael Watson for your feedback and assistance along the way.

I owe a great debt of thanks to Oxford University Press, and especially to my editor, Norman Hirschy, whose immediate support and ongoing enthusiasm for this book provided me with much-needed energy through-out the long writing and editing process, and to Mary Jo Rhodes, whose patience and attention to any questions I might have were so greatly valued and appreciated.

To my partner, Noriko Saito, for your assistance with the photography, for your confidence in me and this project, for your patience and under-standing throughout the long writing process, and for your support in so many ways, a profound thank you.

And finally, I thank my mother and my late father who, apart from their love and support, introduced me to great music, the visual arts, theater, and literature from a very young age. They instilled in me a deep respect and love of the arts, and in so doing, gave me a gift that comforts, enriches, and endures for a lifetime.

INTRODUCTION

For many music teachers, nothing poses a greater mystery than incorporating percussion into the school band or orchestral program.

Sharing no physical relationship with any of the woodwind and brass instruments, the varied assortment of drums, cymbals, keyboards, shakers, and whatnot that constitute the percussion world would appear to have been parachuted in from another planet.

And when it comes to playing percussion, of course, techniques haven't the *slightest* relation to those of the other instruments.

As the rest of the class struggles with their embouchures, breath support, scales, and arpeggios, the percussionists must come to grips—so to speak—with rolls, strange rudiments called "flams" and "paradiddles," and complex coordinations of hands and feet when performing jazz, rock, and Latin rhythms on drum set. Playing timpani—with its music written in bass clef and notes tuned with a foot pedal—presents a whole new set of challenges, and when it comes to sight-reading, no one who has valves and keys at their fingertips understands the plight of the poor xylophone players who, struggling to accurately strike keys just below their line of vision, risk whiplash as their heads bob up and down from music to keyboard and back again.

As if all this weren't enough for classroom teachers to deal with, there's the persistent concern with how to keep percussionists engaged and challenged when the method books—particularly during those first, crucial months—provide them with far too little to do.

And we haven't yet addressed the unique demands of percussion evaluation. With many teachers unsure of what to look and listen for during play tests, it's no wonder that a significant number of students want to learn percussion because it's "easy." Having a xylophonist plunk out a B-flat scale at a snail's pace, for example, presents nowhere near the challenge that a trumpeter faces having to perform the same exercise. Testing drummers on *any* piece that consists of quarter or eighth notes at a tempo that is appropriate for the rest of the class is just one more gift commonly presented to beginning percussionists.

In writing *The Band Teacher's Percussion Guide,* it was of the utmost importance that the finished product be more than just another primer on how to play percussion instruments. While at its most basic level the handbook and companion website that compose *The Band Teacher's Percussion Guide* provide a clear and comprehensive guide to orchestral percussion and drum set techniques, what makes the *Guide* truly unique is its focus on how best to *teach* these fundamentals to percussion students.

To that end, the dozens of exercises throughout the book that focus on performance techniques are accompanied by helpful boxes that, under the headings *What to watch for* and *What to listen for,* provide specific guidelines for both teaching the material and evaluating it. Helpful teaching tips are peppered throughout the book, as are proven teaching methods that I have used successfully with my own students.

Another valuable teaching aid is presented in the form of "lifts and levels," a snare drum performance technique that has multiple benefits: aside from leading to a more relaxed approach to playing snare drum and a clearer connection between the height from which the stick is dropped and the volume of the note, it also provides music teachers with a method of shaping students' playing through simple directions from the podium.

Every effort has been made to prepare teachers for common problems encountered in students' playing, and how best to deal with them when they arise. With chapters and suggestions on how to help keep your percussionists more productively engaged—especially when the method book presents them with minimal challenge—as well as on instrument repair and upkeep, how to select your percussion students, and even classroom organization, the *Guide* strives to be a comprehensive primer for classroom music teachers at any stage of their career.

All technical exercises included in the book have been reproduced in an enlarged format on the *Guide's* companion website, ready to be copied and handed out to students.

Teachers will find that the videos on the companion website will help them grasp performance concepts and teaching suggestions more clearly, and enable them to present material with greater confidence. But students too will benefit from the website by watching and listening to the presentations and modeling their playing after the various demonstrations.

Teaching percussion in the classroom need not be a source of fear. It is my hope that *The Band Teacher's Percussion Guide* will serve as a dependable resource for teacher and student alike, setting the groundwork for a successful and rewarding classroom experience.

ABOUT THE COMPANION WEBSITE

The companion website that accompanies *The Band Teacher's Percussion Guide* can be accessed at

www.oup.com/us/bandteacherspercussionguide

The website includes a series of video presentations demonstrating aspects of material discussed in the book. It is recommended that they be viewed by both percussion students and teachers. All exercises in the *Guide* are also reproduced and enlarged here. Listed by chapter, they may be printed and handed out to students whenever needed. A list of links to online educational resources and performances is also included, as well as material outlining how to knot crash cymbal straps and how to attach cymbals to the hi-hat clutch.

Online material related to the text is indicated with the icon ⏵.

PART 1

Getting Organized

CHAPTER 1.1

Selecting Your Percussionists

There's good reason beginning music students find percussion so seductive.

The sheer variety of sounds—from the subtle ring of a triangle to the snap of a snare drum to the overwhelming roar of the timpani—is jaw-dropping. Add to that the melodic capabilities of the mallet instruments and the power and rhythmic energy of congas and drum sets, and this unique combination of instruments creates a package that is undeniably compelling.

Just keep in mind that percussion is also attractive to students for reasons that are decidedly less than musical.

For some students, "percussion" means "drum set," and they are attracted to drums because they think they are "cool"—which they are. But they also think that since they don't have to struggle to get a sound, and they don't have to play scales and read pitches like other instrumentalists, that playing drums/percussion is easy—which it isn't.

While students may choose to play percussion for the wrong reasons, teachers too often steer students into the percussion section for reasons that are far from prudent. What teachers *shouldn't* do, for example—for reasons outlined later—is stick the student who they most want out of their hair on bass drum . . . or snare drum, timpani, or cabasa for that matter.

Choosing your percussion students is one of the most important decisions you can make with regard to classroom management, the success of your band, and your mental well-being. A wrong decision can haunt you for years.

WHAT TO LOOK FOR IN A PERCUSSIONIST

The ideal percussionist is a serious student of music who can work independently, a good listener who is not craving attention, and someone with proven talent. For sure, these are all desirable qualities regardless of the instrument being played, but keep in mind that the percussionist who can't play rock-solid rhythms and follow the conductor will throw the whole band out of whack; whoever plays four beats to the bar on the concert bass drum wields more control over the orchestra than anyone—including the conductor. You need someone you can trust playing that part.

Your percussionists must be resourceful; they often have to find creative ways to cover as many percussion parts as possible when there aren't enough players.

They must be patient and able to sit quietly when they are not playing; no instrumentalist is left to his or her own devices more often, or for longer periods of time, than the percussionist.

They also, more than any other instrumentalist, must be organized and respectful of the instruments themselves. The instruments—especially the small, Latin percussion instruments—are often lost, misplaced, or simply abused. It's not unusual to see percussion drawers and storage units filled with broken junk.

There is much to think about when choosing your percussionists, and we have a few options to choose from that will help us best gauge which students fit the bill.

THE SELECTION PROCESS
Option One: No Percussion until the Winter Break

If you're in year one of an instrumental music program and don't know the students coming into your class, there's no need to let *anyone* play percussion. Those who request percussion start off playing their second instrumental choice. This gives you time to decide their fate based on their classroom performance. By Winter Break you'll have a pretty clear idea as to who is capable of handling the responsibility.

This approach has further advantages. Those first few weeks playing percussion can be slow going. While the other students in the class are struggling with their new instruments, the percussionists, with only the method books to play from, don't have a lot to challenge them. Even if they are learning the mallet instruments, the exercises at that level are not terribly engaging (see chapter 1.3, *Challenging the Beginning Percussionist*).

Starting percussion a little later ensures that *all* your students will be fully involved in the beginning classes. At the same time, your percussion hopefuls will be learning, or reinforcing, their understanding of notation, which will help with their mallet and timpani playing. When the time comes for the successful candidates to switch to percussion, they should easily be able to catch up to the rest of the class in the method book. An added advantage is that, with the other students now capable of working more independently, you can monitor the percussionists more closely to start them off on the right foot.

Option Two: Auditioning on Percussion

If you do intend to include percussion at the beginning of the year, you might want to try giving the candidates an audition.

You can have them

- play quarter notes as they follow your beat;
- play quarter notes as you change tempos;
- play quarter notes with one hand and eighth notes with another;
- play back rhythmic, two-bar phrases that you tap out; or
- sing a note that you play on piano if you intend for them to play timpani.

Of course, this will not give you all the information you need to make your decision. Throughout this process you will have to observe whether the student has the maturity and listening skills needed to be a successful percussionist.

Option Three: Audition Students Entering from Your Lower School Music Program

Schools with a solid primary music program are able to direct students even more seamlessly into an instrumental middle school program, and students given a keyboard, recorder, or ukulele background in lower grades will be better prepared for, and perhaps more open to, the challenges of playing both nontuned and tuned percussion.

The other big advantage is that you can discuss students' strengths and musical aptitude with their primary teacher in the last weeks of the year before they enter your instrumental program. It also provides an opportunity to spend a short time to audition percussion hopefuls as described in "Option Two" earlier—as well as to check the size, embouchure, and musical background of each of the incoming students to help steer them toward the instrument they are best suited for.

CONCLUSION

Your ideal percussionist is someone who combines musical talent with mature social skills and self-discipline.

However you decide to select your percussionists, it's a decision you should not take lightly.

Planning Your Percussion Program

Once you've selected your percussionists, you face a decision that you'll have to live with for a long time: what instruments will they be required to play? It may sound like a pretty obvious question, but not addressing it, and not working out the implications of your choice, will lead to confusion and frustration for both you and your students.

THE OPTIONS

The fundamental question to ask when planning your program is this: will *all* my percussionists have to learn *all* the main percussion instruments—snare drum, mallets, and timpani? If not, you're left with two other options: will one or more members of the section be your mallet and/or timpani specialists while the others work on nontunable percussion only, or will all the percussionists be allowed to play nontunable percussion while another member of the band—someone with a background in piano—plays the mallet parts when they come up? (Keep in mind that with this second option, even the finest pianists will have difficulty producing good-sounding rolls and playing more advanced timpani and mallet parts.)

Just remember that whatever choice you make, you must be clear in your expectations and consistent with their implementation. If you've decided that your percussionists must play snare drum, mallets, and timpani, you must be sure to divide the students' classroom time among all the instruments and regularly evaluate their playing on each of them.

This last option trains the most well-rounded musician, and for that reason I think it's the best way to go—though the road to success is not obstacle free.

Training the Complete Percussionist:
The Pros and Cons

There are important advantages in having students play all the percussion instruments:

- They have more playing opportunities when exercises or concert music is lightly scored for percussion.
- All the scored parts are always covered (rather than having to leave out the mallet or timpani parts because no one can read the music).
- Your students are able to relate any theory you're teaching to an instrument they actually play.
- You are training well-rounded musicians, capable of reading pitches on a staff, as well as rhythm.

Unfortunately, the goal of developing a well-rounded musician comes with certain challenges—the biggest often being students' resistance to playing anything other than drums (see chapter 4.1, *Introduction: The Mallet Instruments*).

One point that *the resisters* will put forward, however, must be considered seriously: "How," they ask, "can we be expected to play instruments that we can't take home to practice?"

It's a point well taken, and the solution you come up with should have a serious impact on your expectations of their performance.

If we expect students to practice at home to make reasonable progress on an instrument, then we can expect no less when it comes to those playing mallet instruments and timpani. While it's true that your percussionists might be able to learn simpler mallet or timpani parts well enough in class to get by, when it comes to developing the skills to play more demanding music, they'll need access to instruments outside of class—which means quiet time on their own to practice in the music room or practice room. To that end, post a sign-up schedule so percussionists can practice mallets and timpani during recess, during lunchtime, or before or after school. The added benefit? Any quality, one-on-one time you can spend with your percussionists while they are practicing will go a long way to ensuring more successful band classes/rehearsals later on.

THE IMPORTANCE OF THE KEYBOARD

Even if you don't make mallet instrument performance a requirement, I recommend you require your students to have a good basic knowledge of the keyboard. Keep a diagram of the piano keyboard displayed prominently in the classroom so that *all* students can clearly see the relationships between tones and semitones, keys, and so forth.

Those who don't play mallet instruments and who never have to deal with key signatures or pitches are at a huge disadvantage when it comes to understanding the most basic concepts of theory. While you ultimately may not require them to *play* mallet instruments, these instruments should be used as tools to facilitate the understanding of theory and to work out exercises. Even rudimentary familiarity with a mallet instrument will provide students with a window to greater musical understanding.

Assess Your Situation

Many teachers begin percussion programs with the greatest of intentions, only to end up giving in to students who won't make the leap to playing "percussion." Often it's the only viable option to take. By not giving in, you run the risk of losing your percussionists as soon as they are able to drop music—not to mention the fact that your unhappy percussionists can create an unpleasant classroom situation.

So what to do? Unfortunately, there isn't one answer to fit all situations.

While it's clear that training the "complete" percussionist is ideal, being adamant about it, under any circumstance, is clearly a mistake. You have to remain flexible. Your specific situation will dictate the demands you can make upon your students.

Challenging the Beginning Percussionist

Is it any surprise that the beginning percussionist, playing exclusively from the band method book for the first weeks of class, is disengaged and bored?

Compared to the rest of the class, which is absorbed by the process of learning fingerings, breath control, and tone production, percussionists are asked to tap quarter notes on their instruments—and slowly at that. The drummers can, if not watched carefully, play the required notes by clutching the sticks any way they choose, and often get away with learning little or no technique. The same goes for mallet exercises at this stage of the game: it's easy to play a single note on the xylophone, and students will hit the required notes without ever learning a proper approach to "playing" the instrument.

Given little to do or think about, it's not hard for percussionists to feel relegated to the periphery of the learning experience.

But this need not be the case. There are a number of simple ways you can involve your percussionists in the class—and provide them with a richer musical experience—right from the start.

TEACH TECHNIQUE FROM THE BEGINNING

The first weeks of playing provide a valuable opportunity for your students to start thinking critically about their grip and stroke. Although the music at this point requires no real technical challenge, inform them that they will only be able to play more demanding music by practicing and developing a good technique right from the beginning.

Make sure you're familiar with the technical basics (outlined in chapters 2.2, *Holding the Sticks*; 2.3, *The Relaxed Stroke*; and 4.2, *Holding the Mallets*) and consistently remind your percussionists about the following points, which apply to all drumming and mallet playing:

- *Drop* the stick/mallet, don't *hammer* it into the drum.
- Volume corresponds to the height from which the stick/mallet is dropped (so don't hammer into the instrument to get more volume).
- When playing at a consistent volume, the sticks/mallets should be dropped and returned to the same height.
- The sticks/mallets should move straight up and down. Strokes played from the side waste motion and hinder control. Keeping the hands relatively flat and forming a "V" with the sticks/mallets leads to a stroke that moves straight up and down.
- When playing drums, students must listen for an even sound, striking the head in areas that sound the same, at spots that are equidistant from the center.
- Shoulders and arms must be relaxed!

KEEP QUARTER NOTES INTERESTING

There is much that can be done with the material in the method books to keep the first few weeks interesting, especially with the snare exercises. Mallet instruments don't offer as many creative possibilities when it comes to relieving the tedium of reading repeated quarter notes, but having your percussionists play mallets at all can keep them more engaged.

Here are a few suggestions for what you can do to make beginning classes more challenging, interesting, and musical experiences.

Elaborating on Snare Drum Exercises

- Exercises with whole notes, half notes, and/or quarter notes can be played on a suspended cymbal, crash cymbals, a triangle, or a bass drum rather than a snare drum. The goal is to make sure students dampen accurately at the end of each note value.
- Bars of quarter notes can be played with different stickings:
    1. Alternating hands
    2. All right handed
    3. All left handed
    4. Double stroked

5. Paradiddle stickings (right-left-right-right | left-right-left-left)
- Introduce dynamics. Get the students to play alternate bars of mezzo forte and piano.
- Have them play the rhythm on two different instruments at the same time—a pair of toms, a snare and a suspended cymbal, a triangle and a cymbal, and so forth—listening for balance and that they hit the instruments at *exactly* the same time.
- Have them play two different tom-toms, with each hand playing alternate bars on a different instrument.
- Have them play four quarter notes on the suspended cymbal with the right hand, and the written quarter note rhythm with the left hand on the snare drum.

Note: The following exercises develop coordination and timekeeping. They are not reading exercises. They are to be played while the rest of the class reads from the method book.

- Start your students on drum set coordination, having them play
    1. quarter notes on every beat on a closed hi-hat or cymbal with their right hand, along with quarter notes on beats two and four on the snare drum with the left;
    2. quarter notes on every beat using the right foot on the bass drum pedal, along with quarter notes on two and four with the left foot on the hi-hat (sitting for this one);
    3. a combination of #1 and #2: quarter notes on the bass drum and cymbal on every beat, while the snare and hi-hat are played on beats two and four; or
    4. eighth notes on the closed hi-hat or cymbal—not a difficult task even though eighth notes are not introduced in the method book until later on. Shortly after that, you can introduce your percussionists to a simple rock beat, or elements of a rock beat, like that in Example 1.3a. They can accompany the class by playing eighth notes on the closed hi-hat or cymbal, with beats two and four on the snare. Finally, they can add beats one and three on the bass drum.

Example 1.3a

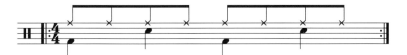

Elaborating on Mallet Instrument Exercises

- After playing the music as written, students can try rolling on each note for the length of its time value (see chapter 4.3, *Playing Mallet Instruments*).
- Have your percussionists play mallet parts keeping their eyes on the music and never looking down at the instrument (see chapter 4.4, *Sight-Reading on Mallet Instruments*). Being conscious now of the importance of developing good reading skills will make a huge difference in their performance later on.

You may come up with ways of your own to help keep your percussionists engaged during the first weeks of class. Just keep in mind that, while the method book is a valuable resource, it can't be relied upon exclusively to provide your percussionists with a musical challenge.

PART 2

The Snare Drum

CHAPTER 2.1

Introduction

The Snare Drum

The importance of offering clear guidance and setting precise goals with regard to your snare drummers' technical development cannot be overstated.

Too often students, even those who have been taking lessons or playing for two or three years, come to me without a clue as to how to hold the sticks: their hands are cramped, their arms and shoulders are tense, the sticks are gripped like baseball bats . . . and with little control over their playing, we're forced to go back to square one and work on basic technique.

It's a discouraging and frustrating exercise for the student, and my directions are often met with a great deal of resistance. Changing bad habits that are ingrained takes a great deal of effort. To make that effort, the student must have complete trust in his or her new teacher—something that may take weeks to develop. It's so much easier to get it right the first time.

Understanding and following the concepts outlined in this chapter will go a long way toward averting a great deal of struggle and frustration—and bad, uncontrolled drumming.

Box 2.1a

SNARE DRUM AND RELATED EQUIPMENT

- Pairs of matched, 5A drumsticks (5A sticks are a good, all-purpose model).
- A snare drum. The standard sizes that come with drum sets, and are most commonly used in bands and orchestras, are 14 inches wide and 5.5 to 6.5 inches deep. As you might expect, shallower drums provide a crisper snare sound and more "bite," while deeper drums provide more body. (Note: It's highly recommended that you invest more money on a decent-quality snare drum, making sure it has a well-built throw-off that can withstand daily classroom wear and tear. Cheap ones won't hold up.)
- Drum pads. Get your drummers into the habit of warming up on these at the beginning of each class. (There are a number of good pads available. If you want a quieter pad, go with a rubber product. The pads that have a surface that is more like a plastic drum head are fine too, but somewhat louder. Six-inch pads should be fine.)
- Snare drum stands that can hold a drum high enough for concert snare drumming and low enough for drum set playing. (You can find a model that accommodates both concert and drum set playing, but you'll likely want separate stands that work for each purpose.)

CHAPTER 2.2

Holding the Sticks

THE BACKGROUND

Good drumming starts with a good grip. Combined with a relaxed stroke, it is indispensable in the development of a controlled technique.

Different Grips

Students may arrive in your band playing either matched or traditional grip (Box 2.2a). They may have learned to play with finger control, wrist control, or a combination of both. There are a number of snare drum grips and techniques that work, and each has its advantages and disadvantages.

If you're starting a student on drums, or if an incoming student has some playing experience but is still struggling with basic techniques, I recommend the matched grip outlined in this chapter. (My basic approach to the grip, as well as other aspects of snare drum technique, reflects my studies with Elden C. "Buster" Bailey. His book *Wrist Twisters: A Musical Approach to Snare Drumming* explores this material in greater depth.)

If a new student plays with control but employs a different grip, it may be just fine, but you may still need to address important aspects of the approach, making sure that

- the student's playing is relaxed,
- the stick is *dropped* rather than hammered into the drum, and
- the stick's trajectory is straight up and down (as opposed to a circular movement).

Box 2.2a

TRADITIONAL VERSUS MATCHED GRIP

Many drummers still use traditional grip. With traditional grip, the stick in the left hand rests at the base of the thumb and index finger, and on top of the fourth finger, which is curled in toward the palm along with the pinky. The index and middle fingers are curled over the top of the stick.

If a student is learning this grip with a private teacher, that's fine. It developed in response to the angle a field drum assumes when hanging from the neck of marching drummers, and is widely used to this day.

I switched from traditional to matched grip. No single grip is perfect, but playing with matched grip on a drum that is flat seems the more natural and logical approach, and with only one hand position to deal with, matched grip is easier both for the student to learn to control and for the band director to teach.

TEACHING THE FUNDAMENTALS

Think of the drumstick as an extension of the arm: you should be able to draw a straight line from the tip of the stick, through the wrist to the elbow.

The student grips the stick in the following manner:

- The thumb and index finger are placed at the stick's optimal balance point, about one-third of the way from the bottom end. This point, at which the stick pivots and rebounds most freely off the drum, is called the fulcrum.
- The index finger is curled underneath the stick, with the fleshy part between the top and second joints gently held against the stick's side. The thumb, *without squeezing*, supports the stick from the opposite side, as seen in Illustration 2.2a.
- With the stick passing under the center of the hand, the third and fourth fingers, shown in Illustration 2.2b, curl underneath, providing it with a bed of support (Box 2.2b).

The thumb and index finger never squeeze the stick. While the curled index finger provides support under the stick, its secondary role, along with the thumb, is to prevent the stick from wobbling from side to side.

Illustration 2.2a Side view of hand position.

(a)

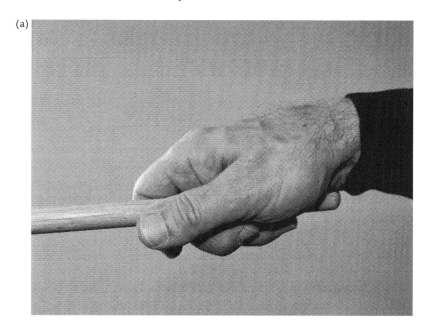

Illustration 2.2b The fingers under the hand.

(b)

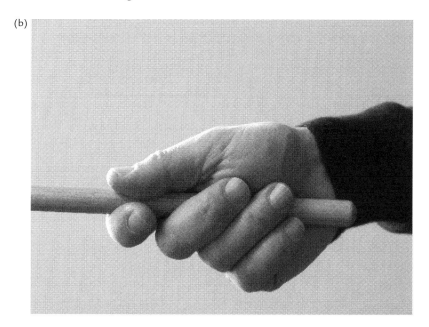

The third and fourth fingers, as shown in Illustration 2.2c, remain curled under the stick, even when the stick is lifted. Illustration 2.2d shows how the fingers are often allowed to flare out, which results in loss of control.

The pinky is relaxed, and dropped slightly out of the way.

Illustration 2.2c The third and fourth fingers support the lifted stick.

Illustration 2.2d The fingers should not flare out when lifting the stick.

Illustration 2.2e Position when standing at the snare drum.

The forearms may be incorporated into the stroke for louder passages, but it's important to note that any movement of the forearm is the result of its *response* to the turning wrist. The stick is *never* lifted with a movement from the elbow combined with a stiff arm and wrist.

Standing at the Drum

When standing at the drum, it is raised roughly to a level 3 or 4 inches below the belt. The shoulders are relaxed, and the arms are tension free.

With the forearm dropping at a slight angle from the elbow, the sticks should be able to comfortably strike the drum just beyond the center of the head.

Illustration 2.2e shows how the wrists are kept low and close to the rim of the drum, and the palms more or less at a parallel angle with the floor. The sticks form a "V" shape.

Box 2.2b
SUPPORTING THE STICK WITH THE THIRD
AND FOURTH FINGERS

When the stick is held with a relaxed grip—supported by the third and fourth fingers beneath it rather than through excessive pressure exerted by the thumb and index finger from the sides—students should feel the weight at the front of the stick pulling gently down on the hand.

To emphasize the support of the third and fourth fingers, have your students try swinging the stick up and down, with the thumb and index finger slightly removed from the stick's sides. They will feel the weight and downward pull from the front end.

The concept of lifting and dropping the weight at the front end of the stick, rather than pushing or hammering the stick down into the drum, is key to the development of a relaxed stroke.

The Relaxed Stroke

THE BACKGROUND

Many beginning drummers think—either consciously or subconsciously—that the faster they play, the more tension they need in their arms, hands, and even shoulders, and the harder they have to hammer the sticks into the drum.

What they don't realize is that they will never develop the speed, control, and fluidity they are capable of through the use of brute force.

To play well, they must develop a sensitivity to the natural rebound off the head of the drum. The ability to do so begins with the development of a smooth, relaxed stroke.

Harnessing the Energy of the Rebound

When a stick hits a drum or cymbal, it bounces back in the opposite direction. But students who play with too much tension, who are hammering the stick into the drum, are not sensitive to that rebound. Because of this, the stick continues to be forced down into the drum *after* it has begun its rebound off the head.

To illustrate, let's look at the effect of this tension on the playing of single strokes.

When a student hammers the stick into the drum and a tense arm and hand are not sensitive to the rebound, the stick is wrestled into the head by a hand still pushing it down when its natural response is to bounce back up. Buzzes creep into the playing. Finally, the single strokes become a series of buzzes—uneven ones at that—and the student has lost control.

The less tension there is in the muscles of the arms and hands, the more responsive the player is to that bounce off the head. What's more, by *incorporating* the energy coming off the drum head into the stroke (see chapter 2.4, *Working with the Rebound*), the student's playing will become quicker and more fluid and relaxed.

TEACHING THE FUNDAMENTALS
Preparing the Stroke

Along with a good, supportive grip, emphasize the importance of a relaxed stroke from the very beginning. The relaxed stroke begins with a relaxed shoulder, arm, and hand. It is something you can help develop by following the *hands-on exercise* discussed in Box 2.3a.

But first, have your students do the following exercise before they begin playing:

- With drumsticks in hand, the students dangle their arms at their sides. The fingers exert just enough pressure to keep the sticks, which are pointing to the floor, from falling.
- They should release any tension in the neck, shoulders, and arms. Give each arm a push; if the arms swing freely, without any resistance, the student is ready to move on.
- The students then lift the forearms from the elbow, bringing the sticks into playing position with the tips just an inch or two above the drum head. The relaxed hand and fingers should be sensitive to the weight pulling down the front end of the stick (see Box 2.2b, page 24, *Supporting the Stick with the Third and Fourth Fingers*).
- The fingers are wrapped around the sticks just firmly enough so that, when playing, the sticks will not fly out of the hand.

With the arm, wrist, and fingers relaxed, the students are ready to play the first notes.

Box 2.3a

HANDS-ON: HELPING PREPARE THE RELAXED STROKE

To make sure the muscles of your student's arm and hand are relaxed, place your fingers under the student's wrist while his or her forearm is at a 90-degree angle to the upper arm. Check that the stick is supported by the third and fourth fingers curled underneath. The wrist should curve slightly downward in response to the weight exerted at the front of the stick. Gently shake the forearm up and down. As you tell the student to relax, you will feel the arm getting heavier as the tension—from the shoulder to the forearm to the hand—is released. This may take some time.

When the arm feels relatively free from tension, tell the student to keep it in that position and as relaxed as possible while you take your fingers away. Next, have the student lift the stick from the wrist, keeping the fingers curved underneath, until the tip (or bead) is raised about 12 inches above the drum. Finally, have the student drop the wrist. The front end of the stick should fall like a dead weight, and the bead will hit the drum. If the fingers remain curled under the hand, and the hand and forearm remain relaxed once the stick has rebounded to about 1 to 2 inches above the head, the student will have successfully executed the stroke. This is essentially the 12-inch-to-2-inch stroke discussed in chapter 2.5, pages 39–41, *Lifts and Levels, From 12 Inches to 2 Inches: The Loud to Quiet Stroke.*

Working with the Rebound

THE BACKGROUND

With the arm relaxed and the sticks in playing position, we are now set to play a series of strokes to develop a feel for that all-important rebound off the drum head. When the upstroke of the wrist is in sync with the rebound, the sticks' motion becomes absolutely fluid. The movement is often compared to that of dribbling a basketball.

TEACHING THE FUNDAMENTALS

To play with a relaxed and controlled stroke, keep the following three points in mind:

- *When the speed of the upstroke is not quick enough, the stick wobbles and there is loss of control*. Students must think of the stroke as being pulled up off the drum rather than being pushed down into the drum. Immediately after the stick is dropped into the drum, the upstroke takes over, with the wrist pulling the stick up off the head in sync with the rebound.
- *Degrees of volume are produced by dropping the stick from different levels above the drum*. Louder notes are produced by dropping the stick from a higher level, *not* by hammering harder into the drum.
- *To play faster strokes, the stick is thrown into the drum more quickly with a relaxed arm and hand*. Beware the tendency to squeeze the stick with the hand and tighten up the arm as the speed increases. Tension leads to hammering into the drum. On top of that, a tense arm is not sensitive

to the rebound off the drum, which provides an energy that should be harnessed and used to the drummer's advantage.

To stay more relaxed as the speed increases, have students focus on executing the quicker upstroke needed to stay in sync with the increasingly faster rebound off the head.

No matter what height the stick is dropped from, the upstrokes and downstrokes should remain fluid and unforced (Box 2.4a).

Exercise 2.4a Practicing single strokes with each hand.

(a)

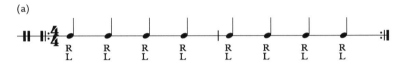

Exercise 2.4a is to be played piano, mezzo forte, and forte.

Exercise 2.4b Matching the sounds of the hands.

(b)

Students play each bar of quarter notes in Exercise 2.4b with a different hand. They should focus on the sticks' position and grip, continually trying to match the weaker hand to the position/grip of the stronger one.

Exercise 2.4c Single strokes: smoothly adding the second hand.

(c)

To practice alternate strokes (the single-stroke roll), Exercise 2.4c requires your students to play quarter notes with one hand while dropping in the eighth note on the half beat every other bar. The purpose here is to consistently monitor the fluidity of the hand that plays repeatedly, and to make sure that the hand joining in on the second half of the beat does not interrupt the "dribbling basketball" feel of the stroke.

Exercise 2.4d The single-stroke roll.

(d)

Exercise 2.4d is simply alternating single strokes. Written here in quarter-note values, it should be practiced at different tempos, or as a series of eighth notes or sixteenth notes.

Rather than starting the single strokes slowly and gradually speeding up, have your students play along with a metronome. As they increase the tempo—and ultimately move from practicing quarter notes to eighth notes or sixteenth notes—the metronome will force them to play evenly, helping them develop an accurate sense of time.

Box 2.4a
PLAYING EXERCISES 2.4A-2.4D

WHAT TO WATCH FOR
- Dropping the stick into the drum from the wrist, rather than pushing or hammering the stick into the drum
- Lifting the stick up off the drum with the wrist
- Lifting in sync with the rebound immediately after striking the drum
- Keeping the third and fourth fingers curved but relaxed under the stick, in contact with it and providing support at all times.
- Positioning the hand and wrist about an inch above the snare drum

WHAT TO LISTEN FOR
- Each note sounding exactly the same

Developing an Even Attack

A consistent problem, especially for the beginning drummer, is that the stronger hand plays more loudly than the weaker hand. The secondary hand struggles to lift the stick as high as the primary hand, and it's not uncommon for the wrist to move in circles instead of making a straight up-and-down motion. As a result, passages tend to be uneven. For the right-handed drummer, the left hand seems to have a mind of its own, and vice versa. (To further ensure an even attack, see Box 2.4b)

A common consequence of one hand playing louder than the other is that two groups of eighth-note triplets tend to pop out like three pairs of eighth notes, with an emphasis on the first, third, and fifth strokes.

Once you've drawn your students' attention to this inequality, make sure that they are aware of its importance. They must raise each stick to

Box 2.4b

WHERE TO STRIKE THE DRUM TO PRODUCE MATCHING TONES FROM EACH STICK

Students often produce different sounds from each hand when striking the head simply because they are playing on two different-sounding areas of the drum.

As the playing area moves from the center of the drum head to the edge, the sound becomes quieter, and there is greater ring and less definition to the attack. As a result, if the sticks do not strike the head in areas that are equidistant from the center, the notes sound different. (Illustrations 2.4a, 2.4b and 2.4c.)

Illustration 2.4a Good stick placement for general to louder playing.

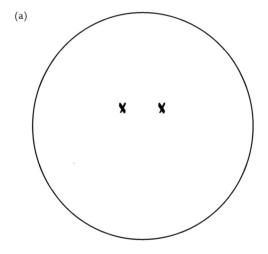

Illustration 2.4b Good stick placement for quieter playing.

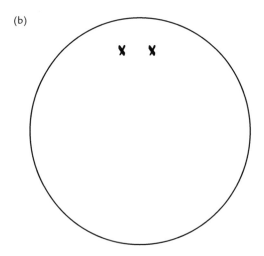

Illustration 2.4c Poor stick placement produces unmatched tones.

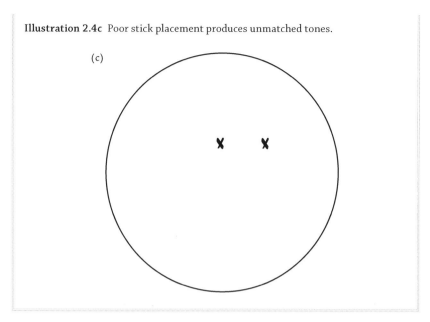

the same height above the drum to play at an even volume. To accomplish this, remind them to *listen to the sound* they produce and to pay careful attention to the height of their hand motions.

Playing with Good Form: A Note on Tests

I would suggest that *a major component of testing should address hand position and the basic stroke*, especially during the early stages of study. It is not enough that your snare drummers tap out quarter notes or simple rhythms slowly on a snare drum. Students must, at this point, focus on playing with good form, and developing the muscle memory and control to perform more complicated material later on. To this end, *a percentage of your marking scheme should incorporate an aspect of technical form*. For example, 25% might be devoted to playing with a proper hand position, or with precise execution of the "lifts and levels" discussed in chapter 2.5, *Lifts and Levels*.

CHAPTER 2.5

Lifts and Levels

THE BACKGROUND

"Lifts and levels" is a system that defines the distance above the drum head from which the tip of the stick is dropped and to which it returns. The study of lifts and levels discourages students from hammering the stick into the drum and losing control, and clarifies the relationship between the height from which the tip—or bead—of the stick is dropped onto the drum and the volume of sound produced. Their practice also helps develop relaxation and control, sets the stage for the execution of tension-free accents, and aids in the fluid performance of rudiments (see chapter 2.6, *The Rudiments: Flams, Paradiddles, Drags, and Four-Stroke Ruffs*). I find that my own students benefit enormously from the practice of lifts and levels, and you can start your students playing them within the first weeks of your program.

The three "levels" in lifts and levels—about 2 inches, 6 inches, and 12 inches above the head of the drum—approximate the points from which the stick is dropped and to which it returns when playing a single stroke. For our purposes, we will limit ourselves to two levels: the 12-inch level, demonstrated in Illustration 2.5a, and a lower level that I will refer to as 2 inches but that you can interpret as meaning anything from 2 inches to 4 inches above the drum head, demonstrated in Illustration 2.5b. *What is important is that levels are consistent throughout each exercise and that there are clear differences between them.*

Depending on which of the two levels the stick is dropped from, the volume of the note produced will be (speaking in very general terms) either quiet to moderate, or loud (for further discussion of dynamics, see Box 2.5a). The level at which the stick comes to rest determines the volume of the *subsequent* note played with that hand.

Illustration 2.5a The 12-inch level.

Illustration 2.5b The 2-inch level.

To illustrate this, consecutive accented triplets, starting with the right hand at 12 inches and the left hand at 2 inches (Example 2.5a), would be played like this:

Example 2.5a

(a)

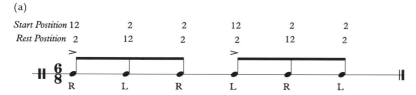

The accented notes are dropped from the 12-inch level, and all the unaccented notes are dropped from the 2-inch level. Notice too how the accented notes finish at the 2-inch level, positioned to play the unaccented notes that follow. The middle note of each triplet, dropped from 2 inches, finishes at 12 inches—the position required to play the following, accented note.

Box 2.5a

PLAYING DIFFERENT DYNAMICS ON A SNARE DRUM

Along with striking the drum from a lower level, one can play more quietly on a snare drum by striking the instrument increasingly closer to the edge of the head. However, playing at the edge also results in greater ring from the instrument and a loss of definition from the snares (and with instruments of lesser quality, that loss of definition is much greater).

Students should play at the edge of the drum when they are unable to play quietly enough closer to the center. (Sometimes, if greater definition is needed when playing at the edge, a handkerchief can be placed over a small area of the head to reduce the ring—a common practice when performing Ravel's Bolero.)

With this in mind, to play a phrase from, for example, pianissimo to fortissimo, your percussionists can begin the phrase at the edge of the instrument and start to lift the sticks higher as they approach the center of the drum. Of course, the opposite may be done when playing from fortissimo to pianissimo.

TEACHING THE FUNDAMENTALS

Many of the points presented in chapter 2.4, *Working with the Rebound,* will help prepare the way for an examination of lifts and levels.

The following exercises are to be played slowly. The time should be free; the student should pause to check levels at the beginning and end of each stroke, which is dropped and lifted with one, fluid motion.

From 12 Inches to 12 Inches:
The Loud-to-Loud Stroke

Exercise 2.5a 12 inches to 12 inches.

(a)

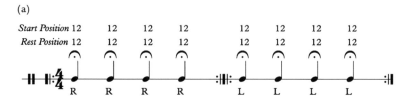

For our first lifts-and-levels exercises, the strokes begin and end at the same level.

Your students will not have much difficulty playing the moderately loud 12-inch-to-12-inch stroke, which is similar to the stroke discussed in chapter 2.4, *Working with the Rebound*. The difference now is that we are separating each stroke to focus on the *precise* height from which the tip of the stick is dropped and, equally importantly, the level at which it comes to rest.

Box 2.5b

THE 12-INCH-TO-12-INCH STROKE

WHAT TO WATCH FOR

- A relaxed drop into the drum
- A smooth lift back to the starting level
- A straight up-and-down motion
- The sticks striking the head at points that are equidistant from the center of the drum

WHAT TO LISTEN FOR

- An even volume and tonal quality from each note

From 2 Inches to 2 Inches: The Quiet-to-Quiet Stroke

Exercise 2.5b 2 inches to 2 inches

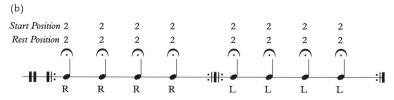

Playing the quiet, 2-inch-to-2-inch stroke requires that the student relax the shoulder, arm, and hand as much as possible. *The tendency to lift the tip of the stick before dropping it must be avoided.* It's an unnecessary motion that defeats the purpose of these exercises.

Box 2.5c

THE 2-INCH-TO-2-INCH STROKE

WHAT TO WATCH FOR

- The stroke drops directly from the 2-inch level without a preparatory lift
- See Box, *The 12-Inch-to-12-Inch Stroke, What to watch for*

WHAT TO LISTEN FOR

- An even volume and tonal quality from each note

From 12 Inches to 2 Inches: The Loud-to-Quiet Stroke

Exercise 2.5c 12 inches to 2 inches

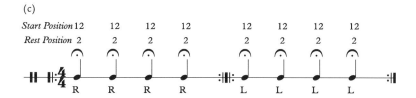

The 12-inch-to-2-inch stroke (introduced in chapter 2.3, Box 2.3a, *Hands-On: Helping Prepare the Relaxed Stroke*, page 27) is one of the most important strokes your students will learn. Having it under control results in a more effortless execution of accents and a more relaxed approach to drumming in general.

To play it, students should do the following:

- Turn the wrist and lift the tip of the stick to a point 12 inches above the drum. Make sure that the fingers don't open up and flip out as the stick is lifted.
- Drop the wrist, allowing the stick to *fall* onto the snare. The hand must stay relaxed and come to a dead stop with the stick resting just slightly above the rim. The relaxed forearm need not move much. It simply follows any wrist movements with a gentle up-and-down motion.
- When the stick hits the drum, the third and fourth fingers remain curved underneath. They should not squeeze the stick. The stick should pop back slightly off the head and stop about an inch or two above it with minimal shaking. *The ability to keep the rebounding stick under control while coming to rest as close to the drum as possible is most important.*

When attempting this exercise for the first time, many students are afraid that the stick will kick back upon hitting the drum and they will lose control. As a result, they often hold back on the drop motion, not allowing the wrist and arm to fall freely. *It is important that they learn to drop the stick without holding back at all.* With a relaxed arm and hand, and with the fingers remaining in position under the palm of the hand, the stick will bounce back and rest close to the drum head.

When playing the beginning lessons in their method books, students playing whole notes, half notes, or slow quarter notes would benefit from playing them this way.

It may take some effort to convince the student that there is no need to tighten the grip on the stick upon hitting the drum, but if the exercise is executed as outlined earlier, the stick will not wobble at all, and you will hear a solid, loud attack.

Box 2.5d

THE 12-INCH-TO-2-INCH STROKE

WHAT TO WATCH FOR

- A tension-free arm and hand
- The third and fourth fingers remain on the stick at all times; they must not flare out at the 12-inch level (the stick remains positioned near the palm of the hand with the fingers curved underneath)
- The hand and stick—with the muscles relaxed and the fingers supporting the stick against the palm—drop from the wrist
- The stick rebounds to the 2-inch level

WHAT TO WATCH FOR

- An even volume and tonal quality from each note

From 2 Inches to 12 Inches:
The Quiet-to-Loud Stroke

Exercise 2.5d 2 inches to 12 inches

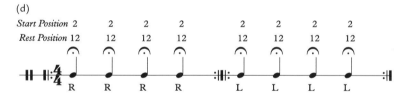

Along with all the points discussed previously, the important thing to remember when moving to a 12-inch position after a 2-inch stroke—to the loud stroke level after having played a quiet note—is not to make a preparatory upstroke before striking the drum. With the hand relaxed and the stick at the 2-inch position, the student must drop the stick onto the head and, in one fluid motion, lift the stick up to the 12-inch position.

You may want to encourage your students to combine the 2- and 12-inch levels with a 6-inch level, but by successfully executing the levels discussed, your percussionists should have a good foundation that will lead to a relaxed, fluid snare drum technique.

Box 2.5e

THE 2-INCH-TO-12-INCH STROKE

WHAT TO WATCH FOR

- A tension-free arm and hand
- The third and fourth fingers remain on the stick at all times; they must not flare out on the upstroke
- No preparatory upswing before striking the drum from the 2-inch level

WHAT TO LISTEN FOR

- An even volume and tonal quality from each note

Playing Accents with Lifts and Levels

Exercise Series 2.5e1–8 Playing accents with lifts and levels

Exercise 2.5e1

(e1)

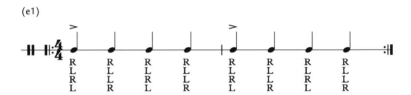

Exercise 2.5e2

(e2)

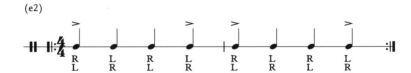

Exercise 2.5e3

(e3)

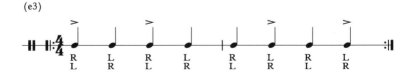

Exercise 2.5e4

(e4)

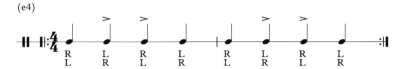

Exercise 2.5e5

(e5)

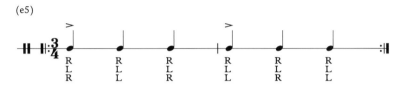

Exercise 2.5e6

(e6)

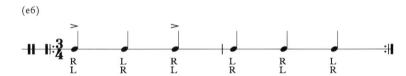

Exercise 2.5e7

(e7)

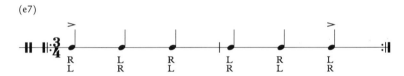

Exercise 2.5e8

(e8)

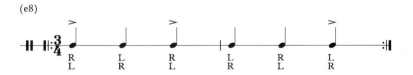

Once students are familiar with the basic strokes, they can apply them to the playing of accents.

Accents often cause beginning snare drummers to panic. They don't read ahead quickly enough to see the accented notes coming. When they stab at them at the last moment, the muscles of the arm and hand tighten up and the rhythm is thrown off. Without any instruction as to how to play accents, your students will continue to struggle with them.

Practicing the previous exercises while giving careful consideration to lifts and levels will lead to a smoother, more relaxed execution of accents.

INCORPORATING LIFTS AND LEVELS INTO YOUR PERCUSSION PROGRAM

As pointed out in The Background section earlier, "lifts and levels" should be incorporated into the percussion program in the beginning weeks of your program.

Once you've introduced your students to the different levels, you can easily provide very clear directions without leaving the podium ("To play pianissimo on beat three with your right hand, make that right-hand note on beat one a 12- to-2-inch stroke"; "Bring the left hand up to 12 inches to match the right for an even fortissimo"). By reminding them of the points to watch for listed earlier—*dropping* rather than forcing the stick down, *lifting* it off the drum, dropping and lifting to a specific height for different dynamic levels and accents, and so forth—you will provide them with valuable direction and help them shape good playing habits at a critical time.

As time goes on and they begin to perform accents, *assign the accent patterns in Exercise 2.5e for short tests*, having your students incorporate lifts and levels when playing them. You can follow that by breaking down rudiments into various combinations of lifts and levels (see chapter 2.6, *The Rudiments: Flams, Paradiddles, Drags, and Four-Stroke Ruffs*).

The Rudiments

Flams, Paradiddles, Drags, and Four-Stroke Ruffs

THE BACKGROUND
What Are Drum Rudiments?

Rudiments are to the snare drum what scales, Czerny, or Hanon studies are to the piano: a practical set of exercises that, if practiced thoughtfully, will go a long way toward developing technical control and dexterity. Developed through military drumming, rudiments are nevertheless practiced and performed today by rock, jazz, and concert percussionists. Though many other exercises and systems have great value, rudiments remain a cornerstone of drum technique.

There are forty rudiments commonly studied today, and serious percussionists are familiar with most if not all of them. They generally consist of accented and unaccented single and double stroke patterns combined with the flams and drags discussed here, the 4-stroke ruff and various rolls. While the individual study of each rudiment lies beyond the scope of this book, by absorbing the concepts behind flam, paradiddle, drag, and four-stroke ruff performance, your students should have the understanding and technical foundation to approach any new rudimental patterns with confidence.

Using Lifts and Levels to Teach Rudiments

By incorporating lifts and levels into their playing, students begin to internalize the relationship between the height from which the stick is dropped and the volume of sound produced. They realize that they don't have to hammer the stick into the drum to play louder. It's a methodology we will incorporate into the teaching of rudiments (see chapter 2.5, *Lifts and Levels*).

Note: The 12- and 2-inch levels are used as guidelines throughout this chapter. They will result in very clear contrasts in volume and will clarify the shape of the rudiments and exercises presented. However, rudiments and other material should be practiced at a variety of volumes, with the height of the sticks adjusted accordingly.

TEACHING THE FUNDAMENTALS
The Paradiddle

Paradiddles are widely used in percussion performance and are among the first rudiments students encounter in their method books.

Concert percussionists use the paradiddle—and variations of it— whenever they need to double a note to make for a more comfortable and/ or musical sticking pattern. Its use also facilitates more effortless movement when multiple percussion is played. It is also widely used by jazz and rock drummers; played in various configurations, it is performed around the set for fills or during solos, and is also used to create rock beats with one hand on the closed hi-hat/cymbal and the other on the snare.

The paradiddle is a four-note sticking pattern that is played hand to hand: RLRR LRLL. It usually, but not always, is written with an accent at the beginning of each four-note group. By applying lifts and levels to this pattern, your students will find that the accent pops out effortlessly in the context of a quick, fluid paradiddle.

Playing Paradiddles with Lifts and Levels

Exercise 2.6a The paradiddle.

(a)

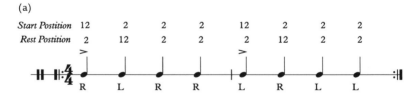

Starting with a right-hand paradiddle:

1. Play the first, accented note with the right stick dropped from the 12-inch position. Since the following right-hand note—the third note of the paradiddle—is unaccented, this stroke rests at the 2-inch position.

2. Play the second, unaccented note with the left stick dropped from the 2-inch position. Since the following left-hand note—beginning the next bar—is accented, this stroke finishes at the 12-inch position.
3. Play the third and fourth strokes beginning and ending at 2 inches. At the end of the first bar, the hands are in position to play a left-hand paradiddle.

Box 2.6a

PLAYING PARADIDDLES WITH LIFTS AND LEVELS

WHAT TO WATCH FOR

- Clearly defined 12-inch and 2-inch levels
- Smooth, relaxed motions between the hands, paying special attention to the second stroke of each paradiddle moving to the first stroke of the following paradiddle

WHAT TO LISTEN FOR

- Consistent accents, played at the same volume

The Flam

Flams consist of a grace note followed by a principal note and, like paradiddles, are used in all styles of drumming.

The names of the rudiments generally provide an important clue as to how they should sound. The two notes of the flam, for example, should be distinct but without too much separation and, when played, should sound something like the word "flam" rather than "fa-lam." The grace note is intended to "thicken" or add weight to the principal note.

Playing Flams with Lifts and Levels

Exercise 2.6b Consecutive right- and left-hand flams.

(b)

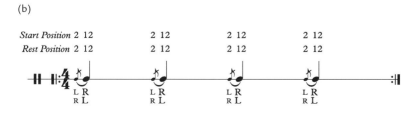

Exercise 2.6c Alternating flams.

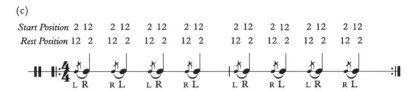

To begin a flam, the sticks are positioned at two different levels: one at 2 inches to play the grace note and the other at 12 inches to play the principal note (see Illustration 2.6a). To play consecutive right- or left-hand flams, as in Exercise 2.6b, the sticks are dropped onto the drum and then lifted back to the levels from which they started. Students should visualize the 2- and 12-inch levels very clearly and practice returning to them with precision. They should become fairly comfortable with repeated flams before moving on to alternating flams.

Illustration 2.6a Starting position for a right-hand flam.

To alternate flams, as in Exercise 2.6c, the sticks switch levels after they are dropped.

Students should stop and check the sticks' positions after playing each flam.

Exercise 2.6d Rhythmic pattern #1 incorporating flams.

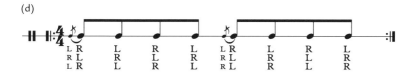

Exercise 2.6e Rhythmic pattern #2 incorporating flams.

Students will come across flam rudiments such as flam accents and flam paradiddles as their playing progresses. These and other flam rudiments - as well as simple patterns with flams such as Exercises 2.6d and 2.6e – should be practiced diligently (see Box 2.6c).

- not lifting back up to a 12-inch level after playing the note at 2 inches, or
- the grace note being dropped from too high a position.

In the first case, have the student focus on dropping the stick, slowing the downward motion, and keeping the arm relaxed.

The second point is corrected, obviously, by focusing on lifting the stick higher. *You can assist your student by holding drumsticks parallel to the drum head at both 12- and 2-inch levels for guidelines.*

In the final case, make sure that, after the 12-inch-to-2-inch stroke is executed, the stick comes to rest very close to the drum head, and that the student *does not make a preparatory lift before playing the grace note.*

The Drag

The drag (sometimes called a ruff) is usually introduced to students in intermediate method books. It consists of a principal note preceded by two grace notes. Like the flam, the grace notes have no time value and are played very close to the principal note.

The grace notes are interpreted two different ways depending on the context. The rudimental drummer will play them open, so that two distinct notes are articulated. Orchestral percussionists will typically play them as a short buzz, though they may open them up to a greater or lesser degree depending on the character of the music being played.

Expect your percussionists to play buzzed grace notes at first as they are easier to execute. Students wanting to play a more rudimental style of drumming, and those simply wanting to refine their technique, will want to practice opening up the grace notes over time.

It's important that the double strokes or buzz be placed clearly before the beat.

Exercise 2.6f Consecutive right- and left-hand drags.

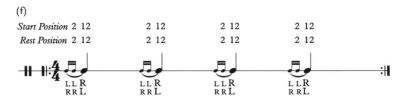

Exercise 2.6g Alternating drags.

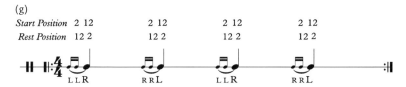

The grace notes must lead smoothly to the main note. There may be a tendency to tighten up to play them—which will lead your snare drummers to jam them into the drum and slow down. *Remind your students not to push the sticks down but rather to keep the arm relaxed and lift the sticks off the drum head immediately after the grace notes are struck.*

As with flams, they should be played in patterns with other notes, and for practice may be substituted for the flams in Exercises 2.6d and 2.6e.

The Four-Stroke Ruff

Exercise 2.6h The four-stroke ruff.

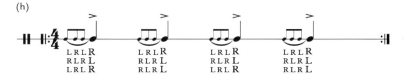

Senior students may be required to play four-stroke ruffs. The tricky part about four-stroke ruffs is that they are played with a single drop of the hands, with a very quick squeeze given to the stick to emphasize the last note.

Box 2.6d

TESTING PARADIDDLES AND OTHER RUDIMENTS

The method books usually introduce paradiddle stickings with quarter notes, which results in students playing paradiddles at tempos that are not much of a challenge. To advance their technique, have your percussionists learn to execute paradiddles at a quicker tempo, one that you have specified on the metronome. Then give them a test.

I strongly suggest you keep this in mind whenever a new rudiment is introduced. Testing the whole class on a line from the method book often results in giving the percussionists a gift. Playing rudiments at a challenging tempo serves two important purposes: it improves students' technical development, and it raises the level of difficulty to that required of the other instrumentalists in your class.

Sticking

THE BACKGROUND

While the rudiments require distinct sticking patterns, the majority of music written for percussionists and drummers alike consists simply of notes on a page, and, like piano fingerings, the choice of sticking patterns is left up to the individual musician.

By the time students are required to play combinations of eighth and sixteenth notes a little more quickly, sticking patterns become an important consideration.

When it comes to choosing stickings, though, there is no simple answer—no single rule that fits all situations, nor one that is the best choice for all percussionists. Ultimately, the best sticking is the one that allows the percussionist to play the passage musically and with the least amount of effort.

Alternate Sticking versus Right-Hand Lead

There are two general approaches to sticking: alternate sticking, where the strokes always move from hand to hand, and playing what is called right-hand or left-hand lead (which we will simply call right-hand lead from now on), a sticking that favors the playing of strong beats with the dominant hand and requires some doubling of strokes. For professionals, and even more so for students struggling with control of the nondominant hand, this often leads to phrases that flow more smoothly.

When students with a weak nondominant hand play certain patterns with alternate stickings, the dominant hand might easily chop up the phrase, placing accents on notes where they don't belong and breaking up the natural rhythmic pulse of the bar (see Examples 2.7a and 2.7b). While right-hand lead stickings on their own won't lead to perfect rhythmic phrasing, playing the downbeats with the dominant hand will often result in students executing snare parts more smoothly and musically.

In Example 2.7a we see what a line might sound like played by a student with a stronger dominant hand using alternate sticking. The unintended accents break up the flow.

(a)

Example 2.7b shows how, with right-hand lead, the accents are not as pronounced on the weaker beats.

(b)

Another advantage to right-hand lead is that, with specific stickings assigned to written patterns, it leads to better sight-reading.

Just keep in mind that as we discuss the benefits of right-hand lead in performance, we must always encourage students to practice technical exercises leading with each hand, with the goal being to equalize the control and power of the two sides.

TEACHING THE FUNDAMENTALS

To explain right-hand lead, we first look at repeated quarter-, eighth-, and sixteenth-note values played with alternate sticking (Examples 2.7c, 2.7e and 2.7g). Removing any of the notes within each pattern, either by replacing them with rests or changing note values, while maintaining the same note-stick relationship leaves us with a right-hand lead sticking (Examples 2.7d, 2.7f and 2.7h).

For example, with consecutive quarter notes as our guide,

(c)

A broken quarter-note pattern is played like this:

(d)

With eighth notes as our guide,

(e)

a broken eighth-note pattern is played like this:

(f)

With sixteenth notes as our guide,

(g)

a broken sixteenth-note pattern is played like this:

(h)

With bars that incorporate combinations of note values (Example 2.7i), it becomes necessary to break up the bar into groups of note values and interpret the sticking accordingly:

(i)

Your percussionists may, at times, prefer to play a sticking other than a right-hand lead sticking—and it will be hard to argue the point if the result is a good-sounding phrase the student is comfortable perform-ing. As pointed out earlier, the bottom line is whether it works musi-cally and technically. Nevertheless, I recommend that students practice the patterns in Exercises 2.7a through 2.7f and become comfortable with them. Follow this up by assigning a piece that incorporates patterns like these (Ted Reed's *Syncopation* is a great resource for this kind of material). If students give it a chance, I have little doubt that they will recognize the benefits of playing right-hand lead and incorporate it into their playing.

Exercise 2.7a Right-hand lead: eighth-note pattern #1

(a)

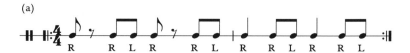

Exercise 2.7b Right-hand lead: eighth-note pattern #2

(b)

Exercise 2.7c Right-hand lead: eighth-note pattern #3

(c)

Exercise 2.7d Right-hand lead: sixteenth-note pattern #1

(d)

Exercise 2.7e Right-hand lead: sixteenth-note pattern #2

(e)

Exercise 2.7f Right-hand lead: sixteenth-note pattern #3

(f)

CHAPTER 2.8

Snare Drum Rolls

THE BACKGROUND
Double-Stroke Rolls versus Buzz Rolls

There are two kinds of snare drum rolls: the buzz or closed roll, where each stroke of the stick provides multiple bounces, and the double-stroke or open roll, where each stick hits the drum with two distinct taps. Though the open roll is widely associated with rudimental—or marching—drumming, and the buzz roll is used more with concert band and symphonic drumming, both are commonly used across a broad range of drumming styles, and the best drummers have a strong command of both techniques. It takes a good deal of practice to play a strong, even double-stroke roll of any duration (five-stroke roll, seven-stroke roll, etc.). While your students should begin practicing double strokes from the beginning, they'll be able to perform a passable buzz roll in much less time, which is why method books introduce the buzz roll after the first few lessons. There's no reason your students should not develop both rolls simultaneously.

TEACHING THE FUNDAMENTALS
The Buzz Roll (or the Closed Roll)

The difficulty in producing a good buzz on a snare drum is finding the middle road between jamming the stick into the drum, which shortens the length of the buzz, and not pressing down enough, which results in the stick making several clear taps before settling down to a buzz.

Point out to your students the function of the third and fourth fingers under the stick. With the fingers in a solid, supportive position—keeping the stick close to the palm of the hand but without squeezing it tightly into the palm—students will be able to play a buzz that sounds even and full at the moment of impact with the drum.

Note: Method books often introduce the roll by requiring students to buzz quarter notes, then eighth notes within simple rhythmic passages. There is nothing wrong with these exercises, which are usually performed with a melody played in unison by the rest of the class, but playing through them in class alone is not enough. To develop a roll that is solid, powerful, and controlled, your students must zero in on the buzz itself. They must practice the exercises presented here (along with others), while paying careful attention to the points in Box 2.8a, and listening critically to the quality of the roll produced. Testing the roll a few times throughout the year would go a long way to focusing students' attention on this very important aspect of percussion performance.

Practicing Buzzing

Exercise 2.8a Buzzing with the right hand.

(a)

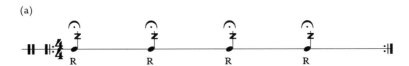

Exercise 2.8b Buzzing with the left hand.

(b)

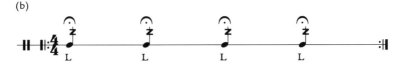

In Exercises 2.8a and 2.8b, we focus on developing as long a buzz as possible, one that distinguishes itself from the open roll from the moment the stick touches the drum. It should be practiced very slowly at first.

Students will have a tendency to speed up, playing buzzes rapidly one after the other. *Don't let them.* The purpose here is to develop a *long, controlled* buzz. And don't forget, the fundamentals of the stroke remain the same: stay relaxed; *drop* the stick—don't *push* it into the drum; and achieve different volumes by dropping the stick from higher or lower levels above the drum.

Exercise 2.8c Matching the buzzes in each hand.

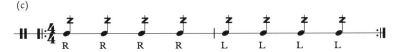

(c)

R   R   R   R   L   L   L   L

The goal of Exercise 2.8c is for students to match the density and length of the buzzes of each hand – which usually involves raising the quality of the buzz played by the non-dominant hand to that of the dominant hand.

Box 2.8a

PRACTICING BUZZING

WHAT TO WATCH FOR

- The third and fourth fingers curled under and supporting the stick at all times (Note: squeezing the stick too tightly against the palm leads to a choked buzz; opening the fingers out and taking them off the stick results in its popping back up before settling into a buzz.)
- Pressing down too hard from the front of the hand, which chokes the buzz
- The same hand/finger positions in both hands
- Both hands lifting the stick to the same height

WHAT TO LISTEN FOR

- A buzz from the moment the stick hits the drum, rather than a buzz preceded by one or more open taps
- Buzzes of the same length and volume with each hand
- Buzzes that are not choked

Developing a Smooth Buzz Roll

Exercise 2.8d Dovetailing the buzzes.

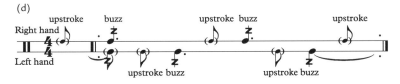

(d)

upstroke   buzz   upstroke buzz   upstroke

Right hand

Left hand

upstroke buzz   upstroke buzz

Once your students have developed some control over the buzz, the next step is to join the buzzes together to create a seamless roll.

Exercise 2.8d is an alternating right-left pattern whereby each stick remains on the head of the drum until *after* the following stick has begun its buzz.

We begin with both sticks resting on the drum. On the pickup to the first bar, the right stick is lifted, then dropped to buzz on the count of "one." On the "and" of one, the left stick is lifted, then dropped to buzz on the count of "two," and so on. For the first half of every beat, the sticks rest together on the drum head.

At slower tempos, the buzzes will not sustain long enough to blend together. At faster tempos, they will begin to dovetail and produce a smooth roll. Note that students must continue to play *long* buzzes as the tempo increases *despite the tendency to shorten them.* The purpose of this exercise is to develop the length and evenness of the buzz rather than the speed of the stroke.

Exercise 2.8d should be practiced at a wide range of speeds on the metronome, starting from MM = 50 to the quarter note. Students should count carefully throughout and give the buzzes their full time value. With a good, long buzz, you should begin to hear a smooth roll at about MM = 208.

Playing Sustained Buzz Rolls with Different Dynamics

When playing sustained, closed, *pianissimo* rolls, students must not allow the arms and hands to get tense. The quietest rolls are played at the edge of the drum. Using a slow, gentle hand motion, students play each buzz as long as possible. The goal is to have the buzzes dovetail seamlessly.

To play sustained, loud rolls, the hand movement will be faster, and the buzzes will be slightly shorter—but be aware of the tendency to play the buzzes too fast and too short! Played this way, the buzzes become separated, making for a choppy roll. To avoid this, see that the stick height is not exaggerated and that the stick is given a firm bed of support with the fingers underneath. The buzzes should still dovetail, and each stick should play a thick buzz while remaining on the drum as long as possible (as illustrated in Exercise 2.8d). Leaning slightly into the drum will help add some weight to the louder buzz.

The Double-Stroke Roll (or the Open Roll)

As mentioned earlier, it takes less time to develop a passable buzz roll than it does a double-stroke roll, and a good buzz roll will sound fine in any context other than that of a marching band. Nevertheless, practicing double-stroke rolls goes a long way toward developing a good snare drum technique, and the ability to play good double strokes is indispensable to the performance of many rudiments and patterns— and, of course, is absolutely essential for anyone wanting to play in a marching band.

Practicing Double Strokes

Exercise 2.8e Double strokes.

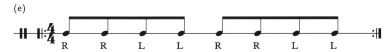

Double strokes—as with most drum exercises—should be practiced with a metronome starting at a slow tempo. Increasing speed along with the metronome, rather than simply starting slowly and getting gradually faster, will help develop control and a good sense of time.

The most important thing to remember when first practicing double strokes is that the second stroke of each stick is executed with a distinct wrist movement and is *not* the result of a bounce. The bounce comes into play only after the double strokes can be played, more or less, as sixteenth notes with the metronome set at around 144.

Get your students to practice on a pillow or folded towel, as well as on a drum or pad, so that they are forced to use their wrists to make that second stroke. If they start to bounce too soon, without first developing the wrist stroke, rolls played at slower tempos will be weak and uneven.

Box 2.8b
PRACTICING DOUBLE STROKES

WHAT TO WATCH FOR
- A second stroke dropped from the same height as the first stroke
- Both hands lifting the stick to the same height

WHAT TO LISTEN FOR
- A second stroke that is the same volume as the first stroke

Exercise 2.8f Accenting the second stroke.

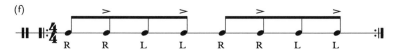

Accenting the second stroke is an excellent exercise for the development of greater control and a more powerful open roll.

Box 2.8c

PRACTICING EXERCISE 2.8F

WHAT TO WATCH FOR

- Two distinct levels, with a second stroke dropped from a higher level
  than the first
- No wobbling of the stick after the accented note hits the drum (see
  chapter 2.5, *Lifts and Levels, From 12 Inches to 2 Inches: The Loud-to-
  Quiet Stroke*, pages 39–41).

WHAT TO LISTEN FOR

- A second stroke that is louder than the first stroke
- Quieter and louder strokes of consistent volumes

Incorporating the Bounce to Play a Faster
Double-Stroke Roll

Once students are playing faster double strokes and beginning to take
advantage of the bounce, you still want to hear a second stroke that is
as strong as the first. For that second stroke, just a slight second wrist
movement is all that is needed to redirect the energy of that rebound
back into the drum. Keeping the third and fourth fingers on the stick
helps keep the rebound under control, keeps the stick closer to the
drum head for a quick return, and allows the drummer to harness
the energy of the upward thrust of the stick and invert it back toward
the drum.

As the roll gets increasingly faster, less consideration is given to making that second stroke. At the higher speeds, one wrist movement—with
support from the wrist and fingers under that stick—is all that is needed
to double stroke.

Measured Rolls

Drum rolls provide percussionists with the means to sustain notes for their full value and allow elements of expression—in the form of dynamics and intensity—to be added to a single note.

The name of a roll (five-stroke roll, seven-stroke roll, nine-stroke roll, etc.) corresponds to the number of double strokes *plus* the final single stroke required to play it. When naming buzzed rolls, two strokes are counted for each buzz.

Unless the number of strokes in a roll is noted in the part—as is common with rudimental snare parts or beginning drum music—the length of a roll is determined by the percussionist. The "right" number of strokes corresponds simply to the number required to produce a solid, sustained snare drum sound through the given unit of time. Deciding on the number of strokes to play in a roll is not an exact science. Much depends on the technique of the player, the tension of the drum, and—for the more experienced percussionist—the quality of sound that the player wants to produce.

However, when measured rolls are introduced in method books, they are presented as either double strokes or buzzes played over an underlying sixteenth-note rhythmic pattern (sometimes referred to as the basic rhythmic pattern, primary stroke, or roll pulse). This system is borrowed from standard rudimental performance/notation, illustrated here starting with Example 2.8a, a quarter-note roll as it would be written in the score:

Example 2.8a

Using an underlying sixteenth-note rhythmic pattern, the quarter-note roll is interpreted as a nine-stroke roll, consisting of four 16th notes either double stroked:

Example 2.8b

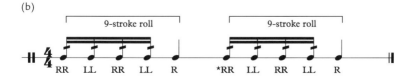

or buzzed:

Example 2.8c

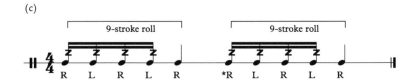

*Note that rolls here, and in subsequent examples, can begin on either hand, with the choice being a considered decision normally left to the percussionist (see chapter 2.7, *Sticking*).

Eighth-note rolls, as seen here:

Example 2.8d

are interpreted as five-stroke rolls, either double stroked:

Example 2.8e

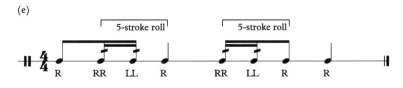

or buzzed:

Example 2.8f

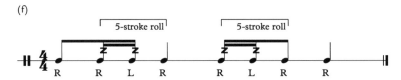

However, while rolling to that underlying sixteenth-note pattern serves much music quite well, it doesn't lead to good rolls at all tempos.

If the tempo is too slow, there will be too much separation between the strokes. To solve this problem, the sound must be thickened by replacing the sixteenth-note rhythm with a sixteenth-note triplet pattern, illustrated in Examples 2.8g and 2.8h with a quarter-note roll:

Example 2.8g

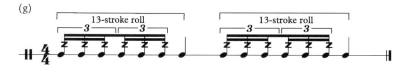

and an eighth-note roll:

Example 2.8h

Tempos that are even slower might require an underlying rhythmic pattern of thirty-second notes:

Example 2.8i

On the other hand, if the tempo is too *fast* to fit in a roll played over a sixteenth-note pattern, snare drummers can use an eighth-note triplet pattern, illustrated here with a quarter-note roll:

Example 2.8j

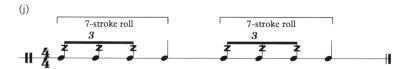

At even faster tempos, an eighth-note pattern will be necessary:

Example 2.8k

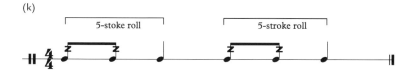

More patterns are available—quintuplet-based patterns, for example—but in most instances, eighth-note, sixteenth-note, and eighth-note and sixteenth-note triplet patterns will provide a solid rhythmic foundation over which to execute rolls.

Note that specific rolls do not correspond to specific rhythmic units. Depending on the tempo of the music, either five-, seven-, or nine-stroke rolls could be used to roll through a full or half beat.

Students should be comfortable with the names and execution of five-, seven-, and nine-stroke rolls, but beyond that it's easier simply to think of playing rolls over the underlying rhythmic patterns discussed here.

Listening for the Final Single Stroke

As well as listening to the quality of buzzes or double strokes in a roll, you must also listen carefully that the single stroke falls exactly in place at the roll's end. If too few buzzes or double strokes are played, there is a tendency to execute that finishing stroke too early. On the other hand, if a roll with too many strokes is attempted—more strokes than the student's technique will allow for at the given speed—the last single stroke may strike too late. In sections of a piece where the roll pattern repeats for several bars—a common occurrence in marches, for example—the playing of that downbeat consistently early or late may force you to either speed up or slow down the tempo to keep the band together.

Box 2.8d
MEASURED ROLLS

WHAT TO LISTEN FOR
- A full, sustained sound for the duration of the roll, with no gaps between buzzes
- The last, single stroke of the roll falling precisely in place

---

Practicing Measured Rolls

The following series of measured roll exercises is notated in quarter and eighth notes for beginning students.

Exercise 2.8g Buzzed five-stroke rolls (eighth-note pattern).

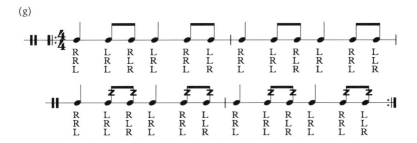

Exercise 2.8h Double-stroked five-stroke rolls (eighth-note pattern).

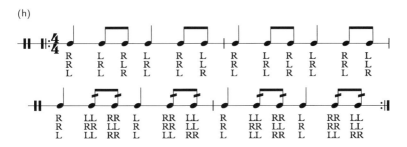

Exercise 2.8i Buzzed seven-stroke rolls (eighth-note triplet pattern).

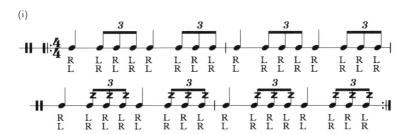

Exercise 2.8j Double-stroked seven-stroke rolls (eighth-note triplet pattern).

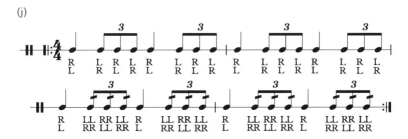

More experienced students, who are familiar with sixteenth notes, can compress the values to eighth and sixteenth notes.

Exercise 2.8k Buzzed five-stroke rolls (sixteenth-note pattern).

Exercise 2.8l Double-stroked five-stroke rolls (sixteenth-note pattern).

Exercise 2.8m Buzzed seven-stroke rolls (sixteenth-note triplet pattern).

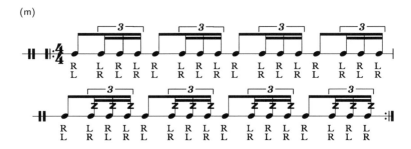

Exercise 2.8n Double-stroked seven-stroke rolls (sixteenth-note triplet pattern).

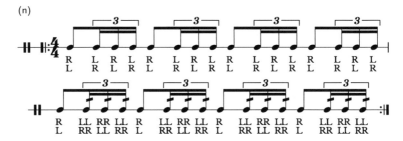

It is important that your students learn to play different rolls at various tempos, as well as learn to start and end rolls on either hand. With this in mind, they should practice all the measured roll exercises with a metronome, making sure that they begin and end each roll with rhythmic precision.

As with new rudiments, when new rolls are introduced in the method book, make the rolls themselves play tests. Require them to be played at different tempos, with students starting and ending the rolls on both hands.

Evaluating Snare Drum Performance

It is important to keep in mind that the exercises and tests that challenge your other instrumentalists don't necessarily challenge your percussionists. As has been pointed out before, playing a single note on a trumpet demands breath control, a trained embouchure, and a recognition and reproduction of pitch. Playing a single note on a snare drum requires that the student drop a stick onto a drum head.

There are, of course, a wealth of challenges when it comes to playing the snare drum well. Unfortunately, they aren't always included in the tests students are required to play. To challenge your students and to effectively develop their technique, I recommend adding one or more of the following points to the method book exercises when testing, especially during the beginning stages:

- Play the test with a metronome at an appropriately quick tempo.
- Play the test with a metronome at a very slow tempo. (Students don't realize how difficult playing at slow tempos can be. I recommend this exercise for *all* your instrumentalists to help develop their sense of time.)
- Reserve a portion of your mark for form (sticks straight up and down, fingers in position, etc.).
- Test the performance of rudiments separately whenever a rudiment is introduced in an exercise. Don't forget to assign appropriate metronome markings as goals.

PART 3

The Drum Set

CHAPTER 3.1

Introduction

The Drum Set

The drum set is capable of generating an excitement unlike that of any other instrument, and drum solos, for better or worse, have been sending audiences into a frenzy since the days of Gene Krupa and Buddy Rich. It's not surprising that, for most of your students, drum set is the reason they're playing percussion.

But contrary to popular belief, electrifying solos are not the measure of a good drummer. First and foremost, the drummer must be a good, steady timekeeper—a fact that all too often is not the focus of students' attention. A good drummer must also develop a keen musical sense, playing figures that are at the service of the music rather than drawing attention away from it. In the hands of an accomplished musician, the drum set and cymbals are capable of creating a rich palette of subtle colors behind a band, as well as infectious rhythmic patterns able to propel instrumentalists of every musical stripe to ever higher levels of performance.

A good snare drum technique provides the foundation needed for playing drum set. Beyond that, the set drummer must develop coordination of the feet and hands, be able to execute rhythms that have evolved from African and Latin musical traditions, internalize the "feel" of jazz and the concept of "swing," have a degree of jazz independence—the ability to play the ride cymbal rhythm while executing other rhythmic figures on the snare and bass drums—and learn to improvise fills and solos around the drum set.

Though it is beyond the scope of this book to provide an in-depth program for the study of jazz, Latin, and rock drum set performance, the exercises presented here will serve as an introduction to those musical styles, as well as help the band teacher identify some of the more common techniques and rhythms associated with drum set playing.

Incorporating Drum Set Exercises into Your Program

There is no reason that, along with snare drum, mallet, and timpani techniques, a component on drum set techniques should not be a clearly defined and essential part of your program. Skills specific to playing drum set must be practiced independent of snare techniques. If your students are required to play drum set in class, or if your drummers play in a jazz or stage band, I strongly recommend that you assign them exercises on jazz independence, rock patterns, Latin rhythms, and fills and solos either from those presented in this chapter or from other sources—and then follow up with a test.

Setting Up the Drum Set

Setting up the drum set is very personal, and there's no single setup that suits the preferences and sizes of all your students (which is why it's important to have a drummer's throne that easily spins to higher or lower levels).

A standard set of drums is generally set up as seen in Illustration 3.1a. In the section titled *Accommodating the Left-Handed Drummer*, alternative setups are discussed.

When setting up the drums, the following points should be kept in mind:

- The throne should be raised so that the drummer's thighs are more or less parallel to the floor or angled slightly downward toward the knee. Sitting lower will make it difficult to manipulate the bass pedal.
- The snare head should be a little below belt height. With the arms hanging loosely from the shoulder and the forearms lifted at the elbow and parallel to the floor, the bead of the drumsticks should reach the center of the head.
- Students playing traditional grip will want to angle the drum down to the right. Students playing matched grip should keep the drum flat, though some may want to angle the drum gently down toward the body. (Allow only a slight angle.)

Illustration 3.1a The drum set.

(a)

- Sitting too close to the drums will cause strain on the leg as the student struggles to lift the bass drum pedal. The leg playing the bass drum should be slightly extended to play comfortably.
- There may be one or two rack toms on the bass drum, set just a little higher than the snare and tilting slightly downward. If there are two toms, the mid tom to the right should be placed so that there is a gentle curve when moving from the rack toms through to the floor tom.
- The ride cymbal is placed at a downward angle toward the drummer, close enough so that he or she won't have to overextend the arm and lift from the shoulder.
- The crash cymbal is placed to the left, between the hi-hat and side tom. If there is only one crash, it should be slightly angled so that it can be played as a ride, but higher than the ride so that it can be struck with the collar of the stick to play a crash.
- The drummer faces straight ahead, in the same direction as the head of the bass drum. There is a tendency for students to seat themselves facing out to the left, with the throne placed to the right of the snare, so that they don't have to twist the neck to read the music. This position

forces the student to pull the right arm too far back when playing the ride cymbal, causing stress to the shoulder.

- With the desk of the music stand placed above the hi-hat, drummers should not have to twist their necks uncomfortably to see both the music and the conductor.

Accommodating the Left-Handed Drummer

The traditional setup for right-handed players places the hi-hat on the left and the bass drum on the right. With the medium and floor tom-toms and ride cymbal to the right, and all the cymbals, including the hi-hat, played with the right hand, the setup favors the right-handed drummer.

Some left-handed drummers reverse everything—placing the bass drum and floor tom on the left and the hi-hat on the right—and play cymbals with *their* dominant hand. A problem with this setup is that when it is necessary to share a drum set (as would be the case in a classroom) or play on a set already set up on a bandstand, they are faced with having to reverse the positions of all the drums and cymbals to play.

Other left-handed drummers have resigned themselves to the right-handed setup and learned to play cymbals with the weaker hand. But there is a third option, "open-handed" drumming, which is the one I recommend.

With open-handed drumming, the ride cymbal is repositioned to the left of the drum set. Other than that, the right-handed drum setup remains in place. The hi-hat and ride cymbals are played with the left hand, while snare drum figures are played with the right. It all makes sense for a couple of reasons: the ability to use the dominant hand to play cymbals is a great advantage, and the whole set need not be rearranged to be played.

I should point out that one doesn't have to be left-handed to play open; right-handed drummers can occasionally be found playing open to avoid the crossover when playing the hi-hat.

Drum Set Notation

The instruments of the drum set are not consistently assigned to the same lines and spaces of the staff, though the drum set key used for this book (Illustration 3.1b) is one that is commonly found elsewhere.

Illustration 3.1b Drum set key.

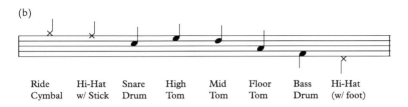

Note heads for drum set cymbals usually take the form of a cross, as in this book, though they may also appear in the shape of a diamond. Cymbal, bass drum and hi-hat notes may appear on a higher or lower line as those presented here, but usually the line designation, and any special symbols, such as those for rim shots, cross sticks and so on, are noted in the score or with a drum set key similar to Illustration 3.1b.

Box 3.1a

DRUM SET AND RELATED EQUIPMENT

- A good student-level drum set. (All the major drum companies man-ufacture drum sets at a wide range of price points, and all have fairly comparable student-level models that will serve you well. As men-tioned before, it's worth investing more money on a decent-quality snare drum, with a well-built throw-off that can withstand daily classroom wear and tear.)
- A drum throne. (To easily accommodate students of different sizes, get one with a seat that spins up and down to adjust it rather than one that must be secured with a screw and bolt.)
- A 20- or 22-inch ride cymbal; a 16- or 18-inch crash; two 14-inch hi-hat cymbals. (Get at least good student-level cymbals rather than the low-end brass cymbals that may be included with cheaper sets.)
- Pairs of matched, 5A drumsticks. (5A sticks are a good, all-purpose model.)
- A cowbell mount for the bass drum may be needed for some Latin music.

See companion website ⊙ for directions and illustrations regarding hi-hat clutch assembly.

CHAPTER 3.2

Drum Set Techniques

THE BACKGROUND

The snare drum technique outlined earlier in this book is a basic and necessary component of playing drum set. To sustain a quick rock, jazz, or Latin cymbal pattern; to play fills on the snare or around the set; or to play rolls, a quick and supple snare technique is called for. (As obvious as this may sound, don't be shocked to find out that some students, after several years of taking private lessons, can barely hold the sticks in their hands, can't read, and haven't the faintest idea how to play a roll. Unfortunately, a vast number of "drum teachers" out there teach how to play beats—and little else!)

The specific challenges to drum set playing—techniques of playing the bass drum, hi-hat, and ride cymbal; coordinating the hands and feet (see Box 3.2a); learning different rhythms and grooves (jazz, Latin, and rock); and performing them idiomatically—are what we will address here.

TEACHING THE FUNDAMENTALS
The Bass Drum

There are two basic techniques used to play the bass drum: "heel up" and "heel down."

Heel Up

"Heel up" is executed by playing the bass pedal with the ball of the foot while keeping the heel up and off the pedal. Depending on the volume

---

Box 3.2a

LEARNING COMPLEX COORDINATION

When learning any rhythm that presents coordination challenges, it is very important to *hear* each part. Students should work out the parts separately, and then experiment with playing them in different two- or three-part combinations before attempting to play all the parts together.

  For example, they might practice a rhythm by breaking it down in the following order:

1. Hands only
2. Feet only
3. Feet and right hand
4. Feet and left hand
5. All together

Emphasize that they must practice *very* slowly while counting carefully— preferably out loud and with a metronome!

---

desired, the heel might be held only a short distance above the pedal or, for louder playing, at a higher distance, with the foot substantially arched.

  A note is struck by either lifting and dropping the leg, turning the ankle, or a combination of both.

  Heel up is more popular among rock drummers. It is more commonly used for louder playing and for playing rapid bass drum patterns, but because there are issues with control at slower tempos and quieter volumes, I recommend that students already playing heel up become comfortable playing the heel-down method as well.

Heel Down

To play "heel down," the foot remains flat on the footboard while playing the bass drum pedal. While there are different views regarding the strengths and weaknesses of heel up versus heel down, my experience is that students playing heel down have greater control of the bass pedal across a wide range of tempos and volumes—and they should have no trouble coming up with all the "punch" they need.

  Having both methods under control allows drummers to achieve as wide a tonal range on the instrument as possible. If drummers playing heel up have difficulties with control or are consistently playing too loudly, have them try playing heel down.

Whichever method they play, be sure to focus their attention on volume, balance, and tone—aspects of playing bass drum that student drummers may need to be reminded of.

Achieving a Good Tone on the Bass Drum

It's quite common for students to bury the beater into the bass drum, that is, leave the beater pressed on the head after it is struck rather than pulling it back off. While burying the beater creates a dry, punchy attack that some drummers, especially rock drummers, find desirable, it's a technique that chokes the drum's tone and produces a "bangy" sound.

I generally prefer the sound produced when the beater springs back off the bass drum, which allows the drum to resonate and produce a warmer, rounder tone.

To do this playing heel down, the leg should be angled away from the drum so that the student can move the ankle freely up and down without creating any tension in the muscles above it. After the beater is propelled into the drum, the ball of the foot pulls back in sync with the beater springing off the head, much like the upstroke of the wrist when playing snare drum.

If you or your students find the bass drum to have too much ring, you may want to put a small pillow or folded towel inside. I would caution against stuffing it too much and making the sound too dry; the sound should be "punchy" with some resonance, not a dull "bang."

Box 3.2b

THE BASS DRUM

WHAT TO WATCH FOR
- Burying the beater into the drum (though this may be acceptable in certain musical contexts)

WHAT TO LISTEN FOR
- A resonant—but not "ringy"—sound, with definition on the attack

The Hi-Hat

Students are often unaware of the sound they are achieving when closing the hi-hat with the foot. It often sounds lifeless, lacking that sharp, rhythmic "chic" that is so important when it comes to driving a band.

A good hi-hat sound is achieved in one of two ways: either by rocking the foot back and forth from heel to toe or by keeping the heel up at all times and more or less bouncing the leg and ball of the foot up and down to open and close the cymbals.

Heel-Toe Technique

I've always played the hi-hat using the heel-toe technique, with the foot rocking back and forth on the footboard. Played this way, the toe pushes down on beats two and four to close the hi-hat cymbals, while the heel comes down on the footboard on beats one and three to release them. Lifting the heel when playing the second and fourth beats in 4/4 time creates a solid "chic" from the cymbals. For softer playing, the heel remains in contact with the pedal when closing the cymbals. At slow tempos in particular, your students will have more control playing heel-toe than with the heel-up technique explained next.

Heel-Up Technique

Playing heel up is another common hi-hat technique. Here, the ball of the foot only remains on the pedal at all times.

With the hi-hat closed, the heel of the foot will hover slightly above the pedal. To play the hi-hat, the leg is lifted up, and the ball of the foot is brought down on the pedal. This technique is particularly useful at faster tempos.

Playing Time with the Stick on the Hi-Hat

(Note: The following discusses the most common technique for a right-handed drummer. The option of playing "open handed" is discussed in chapter 3.1, *Introduction: The Drum Set*, under *Accommodating the Left-Handed Drummer*, page 76).

When playing time on the hi-hat with the stick, as seen in Illustration 3.2a, you have to watch that students don't lift their elbows away from the side of the body, bringing the arm to a position more parallel to the floor. If you find your drummers playing in this position, they must relax their shoulder, drop their arm, then *lift from the elbow only,* keeping the shoulder relaxed, until the hand and stick are at the level of the hi-hat.

Playing the hi-hat with a tight grip and stiff arm often leads to the stick buzzing or double stroking the cymbal rather than playing single notes. Again, the stick must have the freedom to rebound off the hi-hat and the arm must stay relaxed to attain speed.

Illustration 3.2a Arm/wrist position when playing time on the hi-hat.

For those playing with matched grip, watch that the right hand, crossed in front of the body and playing the hi-hat, doesn't get in the way of the left hand playing backbeats on the snare.

If the right hand is directly above the left-hand stick when it's lifted off the drum, the student must move the lower stick slightly to the left. In this position, the stick playing the snare can be lifted in sync with the stick playing the hi-hat, and there will be no difficulty executing a nice, smooth upswing that will drop into the backbeats with all the power and volume needed.

Box 3.2c

THE HI-HAT

WHAT TO WATCH FOR
- A relaxed shoulder and arm with the elbow dropped down
- The sticks positioned so that the left hand can freely move up and down on the snare in coordination with the right hand playing the hi-hat

WHAT TO LISTEN FOR
- A solid "chic" from the cymbals

The Ride Cymbal

Where to Strike the Cymbal

The cymbal should be struck about one-third to halfway between its edge and the bell to achieve a good balance between a clear attack and the wash (shimmer) of the cymbal.

Often, beginners play the cymbal very close to its edge, resulting in a very loud, uncontrolled wash, or too close to the bell, which creates too dry a sound. Sometimes these problems are simply the result of the cymbal being placed too far or too close to the drum set, but more than likely they're the result of students—concentrating intently on coordinating their hands and feet—not listening to the sound they are making.

Holding the Stick

Pushing the stick into the cymbal both kills the sound and leads to loss of control.

To avoid this, the fingers should be curved around the stick with a fairly loose grip that allows the stick a degree of freedom. Unlike the hand position on snare drum, the wrist is turned slightly outward so that the thumb is more or less on top of the stick.

We want the stick to be resting on and supported by the third and fourth fingers, so watch that your students don't pinch the stick tightly between the thumb and index finger while opening up the rest of the hand—leaving no support from the other fingers at all. If the third and fourth fingers remain curled under the stick, supporting *without squeezing it,* the thumb and index finger can relax and the stick will be free to rebound off the cymbal.

The Attack

As mentioned earlier, we want to make sure that the stick isn't being pushed into the cymbal. Doing so can result in some ugly and loud playing.

Your drummers should lift the stick from the wrist and let it fall into the cymbal. If it is gripped loosely enough, it will bounce back off the cymbal. As with the hi-hat and snare attack, the wrist should pick up on this bounce and smoothly lift it back and off the cymbal.

Box 3.2d
THE RIDE CYMBAL

WHAT TO WATCH FOR
- The cymbal struck about one-third to halfway in from its edge
- The wrist turned so that the thumb is more or less on top of the stick
- The fingers wrapped loosely around the stick
- The stick lifted off the cymbal in sync with the natural bounce of the stick

WHAT TO LISTEN FOR
- The balance between a clear attack and the "wash"

The Cross-Stick on Snare Drum

Playing a cross-stick on the snare drum, as shown in Illustration 3.2b, is commonly associated with Latin drum set techniques, though it is also used for jazz, pop, and, less frequently, rock as well.

To play cross-stick on the snare:

- Hold the stick at the front rather than the butt end to get the richest, warmest sound. The bead extends slightly beyond the palm at the base of the fingers.
- Place the thumb and index finger at the sides of the stick.
- Extend the remaining three fingers so that the stick is free to lie flat across the drum.
- Set the palm of the hand on the snare head just off center, with the butt end of the stick extending about 4 inches over the rim.

Illustration 3.2b The cross-stick on the snare drum.

- Holding the stick between the thumb and index finger, and with the rear, outside corner of the hand resting on the snare, lift, then drop the butt end of the stick onto the rim of the drum.
- Listen to the sound. If the quality is thin, experiment with the placement of the hand on the head. The tone quality should have a sharpness that can "cut" through a band without sacrificing warmth and resonance.

CHAPTER 3.3

Jazz Drumming

THE BACKGROUND

Whether they're playing drum set in class or in a stage/jazz band, your drummers will often be required to play jazz . . . and make it swing. For many of them, jazz is like a foreign language: they can say the words, but the pronunciation and accent are all wrong (see Box 3.3a).

When it comes to playing a ride rhythm on the cymbal, they *sort of* know what it sounds like. They approximate it by placing the skip note—commonly written as the last triplet or last sixteenth note of the second and fourth beats of a 4/4 bar—in what they think is the right spot. Typically, though, they place too much emphasis on the wrong beat of the bar or play the pattern too stiffly. Of course, if they don't lay down the quarter notes in the right place, it doesn't feel right at all.

For the drummer, swinging jazz flows directly from the ride rhythm, whether it's played on the cymbal, on the hi-hat, or with brushes on the snare drum. Tied in with the ride rhythm is what is called jazz independence: the ability to both comp—play snare and bass drum accents and patterns that complement and support the soloist—and play ensemble figures on the snare drum while maintaining the ride rhythm with the right hand. It's a very important aspect of jazz drumming that is rarely given the attention that is required.

Box 3.3a

THE IMPORTANCE OF LISTENING TO JAZZ, PART 1

How can we expect students to "swing" when they've only heard rock and pop music all their lives?

Unfortunately, while many students study instrumental music for six or seven years or more, they rarely hear great jazz. They play the notes, but remain unfamiliar with the musical idiom they are learning.

It has never been easier for students to see and hear great jazz musicians and bands, both past and present. If your band is playing a Basie chart, find it—or find something close to it—on YouTube. If they're playing *Sing, Sing, Sing*, how can you *not* play for them the Benny Goodman version with Gene Krupa? Introduce your class to great drummers, from Buddy Rich to Jack DeJohnette, from Jo Jones to Max Roach and Steve Gadd . . . and to other important instrumentalists as well.

By not doing so, a golden opportunity to connect students to the rich musical legacy of jazz and to its greatest proponents—musicians who should serve as a source of inspiration—might be lost forever.

TEACHING THE FUNDAMENTALS
A Swinging Ride Cymbal

Exercise 3.3a Playing even and relaxed quarter notes on the cymbal.

(a)

Ride
Cymbal

Focusing on an even, unaccented quarter-note feel, have your students play quarter notes on the cymbal at about MM = 60. Encourage them to practice Exercise 3.3a—and most everything else—with a metronome (Box 3.3b). (You might want to pick one up for your students to use in class.)

The hand should stay relaxed, without a tight grip on the stick. Playing slowly, the student drops the stick onto the cymbal, leaving it to rest about an inch above the cymbal after the rebound. The subsequent notes are played in the same manner. As the tempo increases, the stick is lifted back up off the cymbal after each strike, seamlessly following the natural rebound.

Remember that the stick should strike the cymbal about one-third to halfway between its edge and the bell to get a good balance between the clarity of the principal note and the wash of the cymbal.

Box 3.3b

PRACTICING THE RIDE RHYTHM WITH A METRONOME

Constantly speeding up and slowing down the ride rhythm while practicing does nothing to develop your students' sense of time.

Have them practice with a metronome at *slow* tempos, making sure that the quarter note of the cymbal beat falls exactly in place. They may complain that they "can't play with the metronome"—implying that it somehow impedes their ability to play. At that point, you just have to tell them that if they can't play with it, they can't play without it.

In my studio, we call the metronome the lie detector. When students finally do meet the challenge of playing along comfortably with the metronome, they will take pride in their accomplishment—and the benefits will be felt throughout your entire band.

Exercise 3.3b Quarter notes on the cymbal plus bass drum and hi-hat.

(b)

In Exercise 3.3b, we add the bass drum on all four beats and the hi-hat on beats two and four.

It is very common for young drummers, used to listening to rock, to play too heavily on the bass drum (Box 3.3c). Impress upon them that the bass drum quarter-note pattern is "feathered"—played as a light pulse only.

Box 3.3c

BALANCING THE DRUM SET

Many students, coming from a background of rock, tend to play the bass drum very loudly no matter what the musical idiom. Thus, Latin music, which also generally incorporates an eighth-note ride rhythm, can quickly take on a rock character. Conversely, the sound of the hi-hat, played with the foot on the second and fourth beats, is often lost in the mix. Ride cymbals may be played too close to the edge, creating very little attack and lots of loud wash, or too close to the bell, where the opposite effect is achieved.

There's a lot to think about when it comes to playing the drum set, and you must continue to remind your students to listen to the sound they are creating as a whole. They must remain aware of the balance of the component parts of the drum set with each rhythm they are playing. With jazz, you want to hear a clear, bouncy rhythm on the cymbal, the bass drum providing a pulse rather than a heavy thump, and the sharp "chic" of the hi-hat cutting through the music.

Exercise 3.3c The ride rhythm, cymbal alone.

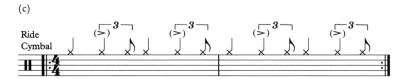

The notes played before beats one and three—the skip notes—should be thought of as pickup notes. They're not as loud as the notes that fall on the beat, and are dropped from a lower level. The drop and lift motion through all the cymbal notes should be very fluid.

Students should count out loud while playing the ride rhythm in Exercise 3.3c to correctly place the skip beat: *1-trip-let 2-trip-let 3-trip-let 4-trip-let.*

The ride cymbal rhythm can also be interpreted with a slight accent played on beats two and four, but this should not be exaggerated. And under no circumstances should accents fall regularly on beats one and three.

Exercise 3.3d The ride rhythm with bass drum and hi-hat.

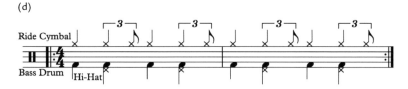

Once students are comfortable with the ride rhythm, the bass drum and hi-hat can be added.

Students must listen carefully to the balance of all the instruments, and that they all play the downbeats at *exactly* the same time.

Have your students continue to count triplets out loud while practicing the ride rhythm. As always, remind them that their role is to keep *steady time*. (Box 3.3d.)

Box 3.3d

JAZZ DRUMMING: KEEPING TIME ON THE DRUM SET

WHAT TO WATCH FOR
- Striking the cymbal about one-third to halfway in from the edge
- The thumb is on top of the stick
- The stick is lifted and dropped from the wrist, not the arm
- The bass drum pedal is lifted back off the drum after striking, not buried into the head

WHAT TO LISTEN FOR
- The four cymbal downbeats are played at the same volume or with a slight accent at the beginning of beats two and four
- The hi-hat makes a strong "chic" sound
- The skip note corresponds to the last beat of a triplet
- The bass drum notes all sound the same
- The bass drum is feathered
- All instruments play the downbeats at *exactly* the same time

---

Playing the Ride Rhythm on the Hi-Hat

Exercise 3.3e The ride rhythm on the hi-hat.

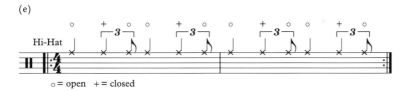

When playing the ride rhythm on the hi-hat, students must be sure that *beats two and four only* are struck on the closed hi-hat. Beats one and three, *as well as the skip beats*, are played with the cymbals open, but only slightly, so that they sizzle together when struck.

It's not uncommon for students to have difficulty closing the hi-hat at *exactly* the same time the stick strikes the cymbal on beats two and four. Make sure they are listening carefully. If they don't get the timing just right, the early cymbal attack followed by the hi-hat "chic" will create a flamlike effect. (Box 3.3e.)

Box 3.3e

PLAYING THE RIDE RHYTHM ON THE HI-HAT

WHAT TO LISTEN FOR

- The stick striking the closed hi-hat on beats two and four only
- The stick striking the hi-hat at the *exact moment* it closes on beats two and four
- A consistent sizzle sound from the two cymbals when the stick strikes the open hi-hat

Playing with Brushes

By and large, playing with brushes is an art associated with jazz drumming. While there are a multitude of patterns available to the drummer, the most basic, shown in Illustrations 3.3a through 3.3c, are used extensively.

All the patterns illustrated here require the drummer to play a ride rhythm on the snare drum with the right-hand brush, while at the same time sliding the other brush over the drum head in smaller or larger circles, depending on the tempo of the music.

Illustration 3.3a A slow to moderate brush pattern in 4/4 time.

(a)

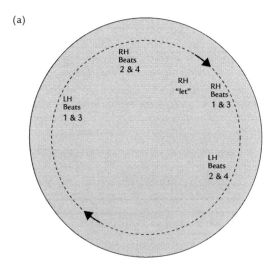

At a slow to moderate 4/4 tempo, the left-hand brush sweeps a large circle clockwise around the outside edge of the drum. The right hand breaks up the ride rhythm across the top of the drum, lifting the brush up and to the left as the left hand sweeps underneath and to the right.

Illustration 3.3b A quicker brush pattern in 4/4 time.

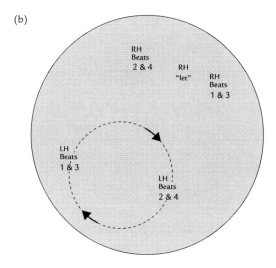

At a quicker 4/4 tempo, the left-hand brush sweeps a smaller clockwise circle in the bottom left quarter of the head.

Illustration 3.3c A brush pattern in 3/4 time.

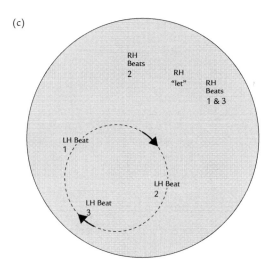

As with the 4/4 patterns, the size of the sweep when playing a 3/4 brush pattern will depend on the tempo.

Learning Jazz Independence

Jazz independence refers to the ability to play independent patterns on the snare drum, bass drum, and hi-hat against a steady jazz ride cymbal rhythm. This can all become extremely complex, but for our purposes we'll stick to the basics.

A degree of independence is needed so that drummers can, as mentioned earlier, free up the left hand to play ensemble figures and to "comp" without disturbing the ride rhythm played with the right hand. Exercises 3.3f1 through 3.3f14 will get your students started. Remind them to pay attention to the guidelines in Box 3.3d, *Jazz: Drumming: Keeping Time on the Drum Set*, when practicing.

The study of these exercises, and others like them, should be a requirement if a jazz/stage band is a component of your program.

Exercises 3.3f1–10. Jazz independence exercises in 4/4 time.

Exercise 3.3f1

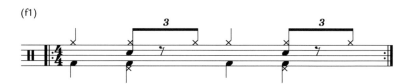

Exercise 3.3f2

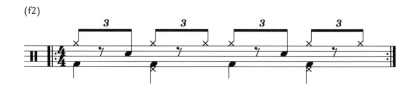

Exercise 3.3f3

Exercise 3.3f4

Exercise 3.3f5

(f5)

Exercise 3.3f6

(f6)

Exercise 3.3f7

(f7)

Exercise 3.3f8

(f8)

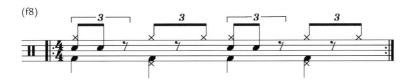

Exercise 3.3f9

(f9)

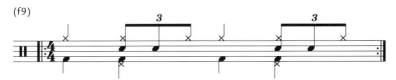

Exercise 3.3f10

(f10)

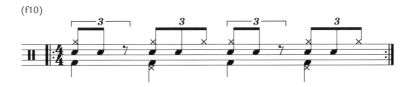

Exercises 3.3f11–14 Jazz independence exercises in 3/4 time

Exercise 3.3f11

(f11)

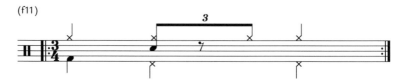

Exercise 3.3f12

(f12)

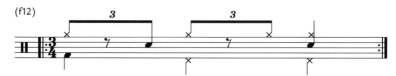

Exercise 3.3f13

(f13)

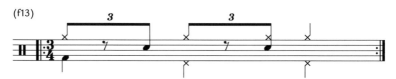

Exercise 3.3f14

(f14)

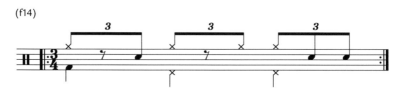

Note: As drumming moved from "swing" style to "be-bop" in the 1940s, drummers shifted from playing all four beats on the bass drum to playing accents on the bass drum. They also began performing more and more intricate patterns between the snare and bass drum while still maintaining the ride rhythm (though to this day many jazz drummers still lightly feather the bass drum on all four beats for a substantial part of the music).

To begin practicing more advanced independence techniques, Exercises 33.3f1–14 can be interpreted

1. with the bass drum playing the snare drum line or
2. with the snare drum line divided between the bass drum and snare drum.

For a creative exercise, your students can combine elements of different bars and divide the parts between snare drum and bass drum, as in Examples 3.3a and 3.3b.

Example 3.3a

Example 3.3b

Box 3.3f

THE IMPORTANCE OF LISTENING TO JAZZ, PART 2: COMPING, TRANSITIONAL FILLS, AND PLAYING ON THE UPBEAT

It's one thing to be able to execute independence exercises and another to be able to use this new skill tastefully and idiomatically when performing.

Keep in mind that it's the accented *upbeats* that propel the music forward. Too often students comp too heavily and loudly on downbeats.

The same mistake is made with fills (see chapter 3.6, *Solos and Fills*). Often the fills that should be placed in a transition within a piece—typically leading into an "A" or "B" section of a tune—are heavy-handed or played in an inappropriate place. At worst, fills are inserted simply because a bored drummer wants something more to do.

As far as transitional fills are concerned, less is more, and a few well-placed notes are usually all that is required—and desired—musically. If a longer fill is called for, then it should be shaped with accents on the upbeat rather than the downbeat like this:

Example 3.3f-a

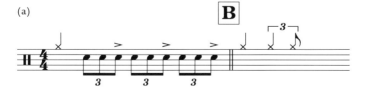

instead of this:

Example 3.3f-bb

(b)

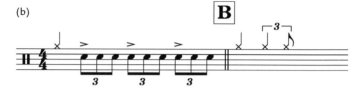

Only through exposure to tasteful musicianship will your students learn to play musically and idiomatically themselves.

CHAPTER 3.4

Latin Drumming

THE BACKGROUND

Most likely, the multitude of rhythms that compose contemporary Latin drumming are completely unknown to the high school drummer.

"Latin drumming" covers a lot of territory, with styles that include mambo, bossa nova, merengue, salsa, rhumba, samba, and cha-cha, to name but a few. They are often wildly different, and the degree of coordination needed to play them can be extremely complex. Presented here is a very basic introduction to Latin drumming—a little background and a few basic rhythms—to help ease your students into this fascinating area of study.

Generally, there are two styles that fall under the banner of Latin drumming: Brazilian, which includes bossa nova and samba, and Afro-Cuban, which includes mambo, cha-cha, songo, salsa and several other forms. The rhythms played on the Western drum set are meant to approximate the often complex rhythmic patterns generated by an ensemble of percussionists playing traditional instruments originating primarily in Latin America and Africa.

Just make sure that your students don't play Latin music as if they were playing rock. Due to the eighth-note feel, there's a tendency to play with a heavy bass drum and hammer the hi-hat with the shoulder of the stick rather than the bead. Bossa nova in particular requires a light and buoyant touch.

TEACHING THE FUNDAMENTALS
Brazilian Drumming

The styles of Brazilian popular music most commonly heard are samba and bossa nova, with the bossa nova in effect being a slower, smoother version of the samba.

Bossa Nova

Exercise 3.4a Bossa nova.

Note that the eighth-note time pattern can be played with a stick on the closed hi-hat or cymbal or with a brush on the snare, hi-hat, or cymbal. It is not unusual to find drummers starting a piece quietly, with a brush playing eighth notes on the snare, moving to the cymbal at the bridge of the tune, and then playing with a stick later in the piece.

The left hand on the snare drum plays cross-stick (see chapter 3.2, *Drum Set Techniques*, page 85.

Samba

Samba rhythms are lively and exciting, and you'll find great variation in the patterns that are played—some of which are extraordinarily complex.

Exercise 3.4b Beginning samba pattern.

*Snare may be played with a brush or stick

We're keeping it simple for the beginning drummer by having the bass drum play quarter notes rather than the traditional dotted eighth/sixteenth samba bass pattern.

Note that the right hand moves between the rack tom and floor tom, while the left hand consistently plays the backbeat on the snare with either a brush or a stick.

Exercise 3.4c More advanced samba pattern.

This more advanced samba pattern introduces the samba bass drum rhythm and more complex syncopation.

More control of the bass drum is needed to play the dotted eighth/ sixteenth pattern with rhythmic precision. To add further difficulty, it's often required to be played at a very fast tempo.

Afro-Cuban Drumming: Deconstructing Salsa

To open a small window into the world of Afro-Cuban music, we're going to deconstruct a basic salsa beat (Exercise 3.4l), a rhythm associated originally with Cuban and Puerto Rican dance music. It is composed of three important rhythmic components: clave, a rhythm at the very heart of Afro-Cuban music played here on a snare drum with a cross-stick; the common cascara pattern, which can be played on the side of the floor tom, closed hi-hat, or cymbal; and the tumbao, played on the bass drum.

Clave

Fundamental to all Afro-Cuban drumming is the understanding of "clave."

The word "clave" means "key" in Spanish, and in Afro-Cuban music it refers to two things: the rhythmic patterns that constitute the foundation of the music, as shown in Examples 3.4a through 3.4d, and, in its plural form "claves", the two cylindrical pieces of wood that are struck together to play those rhythms.

Example 3.4a The 3:2 son clave.

Example 3.4b The 2:3 son clave.

(b)

Example 3.4c The 3:2 rhumba clave.

(c)

Example 3.4d The 2:3 rhumba clave.

(d)

The son clave and the rhumba clave both have three notes in one bar and two in the other.

Since the position of the bars may switch depending on the music being played, bar order is specified by designating them as 3:2 or 2:3 son or rhumba clave patterns.

Exercise 3.4d The 3:2 son clave on drum set.

(d)

Exercise 3.4e The 2:3 son clave on drum set.

(e)

Exercise 3.4f The 3:2 rhumba clave on drum set.

(f)

Exercise 3.4g The 2:3 rhumba clave on drum set.

(g)

When playing clave on a drum set (Exercises 3.4d–3.4g), the drummer mimics the sound of the claves by playing the son and rhumba rhythms with a cross-stick on the snare drum. The beginning drummer can add eighth notes on the hi-hat and quarter notes on the bass drum on beats one and three.

Cascara

The Spanish word "cascara" means "shell," and this important pattern (Example 3.4e) is typically played on the shell of a timbal—the shallow, single-headed drum played in Latin bands—often during the verse or softer sections of the music.

Example 3.4e The cascara pattern.

(e)

On a drum set, the cascara pattern is played either on the side of the floor tom, on the hi-hat, or on the cymbal.

Exercise 3.4h The cascara pattern with 3:2 son clave.

(h)

Exercise 3.4i The cascara pattern with 2:3 son clave.

(i)

Exercise 3.4j The cascara pattern with 3:2 rhumba clave.

(j)

Exercise 3.4k The cascara pattern with 2:3 rhumba clave.

(k)

In Exercises 3.4h through 3.4k, the cascara pattern is played with the right hand, while the 3:2 or 2:3 son or rhumba pattern is played cross-stick on the snare.

Note that when changing from 3:2 to 2:3 clave patterns, the order of the cascara bars is reversed as well.

Tumbao

The tumbao rhythm, played on the bass drum (Example 3.4f), further adds to an authentic Afro-Cuban feel—but be forewarned: when played in conjunction with the right-hand cascara pattern and the left-hand son or rhumba pattern, we're getting into some pretty complex rhythmical coordination suitable for a more advanced player.

Example 3.4f The tumbao pattern.

(f)

The syncopated bass drum tumbao pattern is played along with the bass player and piano player. The pattern must be practiced very carefully as a rhythm section, and then with the other instruments, for it to really "groove."

Putting it All Together: Playing Salsa

Exercise 3.4l Salsa: The 3:2 son pattern, cascara, and tumbao (reverse bars for the 2:3 son).

(l)

In Exercise 3.4l we add the tumbao to the 3:2 son pattern with the cascara pattern in the right hand to play salsa.

Exercise 3.4m The 3:2 rhumba pattern, cascara, and tumbao (reverse bars for the 2:3 rhumba).

(m)

Students can also practice tumbao and cascara with the rhumba clave, as in Exercise 3.4m. (Note that the son clave is used to play salsa.)

Other Common Rhythms

While there are many more Afro-Cuban and world rhythms—as well as countless variations on all of them—here are just a few more that are commonly played.

Exercise 3.4n Cha-cha.

(n)

Exercise 3.4o Songo.

(o)

Exercise 3.4p Reggae 1. (While not Latin, this popular world rhythm is included here.)

(p)

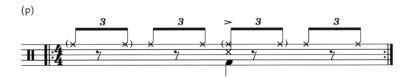

Exercise 3.4q Reggae 2.

(q)

CHAPTER 3.5

Rock Drumming

THE BACKGROUND

You should have little difficulty motivating your drummers to work on rock drumming skills; rock and pop music, unlike jazz or Latin music, is the soundtrack of their lives, and the playing of it is, for many of your students, their prime musical motivation.

The exercises presented here are basic, and just a sampling of the possibilities available to a drummer. They are meant to provide both teacher and student with a simple but practical introduction to rock drumming through the first months of study. Depending on your students' level of experience, these exercises will challenge their coordination skills to a greater or lesser degree.

Unlike military drum rudiments, rock beats are not catalogued. They're called "rock beats," but the impulse behind their inclusion here and in other publications is not unlike that of jazz independence exercises: they train drummers to coordinate and integrate the instruments of the drum set while maintaining steady timekeeping (Box 3.3a) on the hi-hat or cymbal. However, you'll often hear drummers playing some of the patterns presented here—and often the simplest ones—exactly as written.

Rock Timekeeping Patterns on the Hi-Hat and Cymbal

When timekeeping patterns are played on the closed hi-hat, students need only integrate the bass and snare drum parts to fill out the beat, which is often what beginning drummers are required to do.

When the pattern moves to the cymbal, the hi-hat is free to be played with the foot on beats two and four when playing 4/4 time (and beats two or two and three when playing in 3/4 time, a far less common time signature in rock).

While the eighth-note time feel is most often required, students should also be comfortable playing quarter notes and sixteenth notes on the hi-hat or cymbal. I recommend that quarter notes on the hi-hat and cymbal be introduced along with eighths right from the beginning, with sixteenth notes added later on.

Box 3.5a

PRACTICING WITH A METRONOME (... AGAIN)

As the old joke goes, "So many drummers, so little time...."

Several factors can contribute to unsteady timekeeping. The issues may be technical. If students' bass drum technique is not developed, lack of control over the pedal can throw off their time. Their cymbal technique, too, could be throwing them off. More often than not, students are simply unaware of the need to practice solid, steady timekeeping. Whatever the reason, if you ask them to play along with a metronome, the frustration level skyrockets. They often can't do it.

I may sound like a broken record, but everything about the metronome written in the "Jazz Drumming" chapter (chapter 3.3, Box 3.3b, *Practicing the Ride Rhythm with a Metronome*, page 89) holds true here: when it comes to developing good timekeeping—and this goes for all instrumentalists—the metronome is the most effective tool you have at your disposal. *Require* your students to practice and perform the patterns listed in this chapter with a metronome—and don't neglect to assign slow tempos.

TEACHING THE FUNDAMENTALS

Exercises 3.5a1 through 3.5a12 consist of simple quarter- and eighth-note snare and bass drum patterns played against an eighth-note time feel on the closed hi-hat.

Exercises 3.5b1 through 3.5b12 introduce sixteenth-note figures to the snare and bass patterns.

Rock Beat Patterns

Exercises 3.5a1–12. Rock beats with quarter and eighth notes on the snare and bass drum.

Exercise 3.5a1

Exercise 3.5a2

Exercise 3.5a3

Exercise 3.5a4

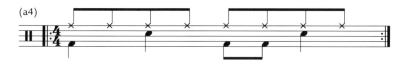

Exercise 3.5a5

Exercise 3.5a6

Exercise 3.5a7

Exercise 3.5a8

Exercise 3.5a9

Exercise 3.5a10

Exercise 3.5a11

Exercise 3.5a12

Exercises 3.5b1–12. Rock beats with quarter, eighth, and sixteenth notes on the snare and bass drum.

Exercise 3.5b1

(b1)

Exercise 3.5b2

(b2)

Exercise 3.5b3

(b3)
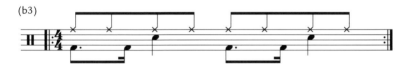

Exercise 3.5b4

(b4)

Exercise 3.5b5

(b5)

Exercise 3.5b6

(b6)

Exercise 3.5b7

(b7)

Exercise 3.5b8

(b8)

Exercise 3.5b9

(b9)

Exercise 3.5b10

(b10)

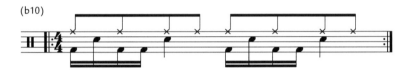

Exercise 3.5b11

(b11)

Exercise 3.5b12

(b12)

Exercise 3.5c is an example of what students can create when combining elements of the previous rock beat patterns.

Exercise 3.5 Rock beat with combined rhythmic elements.

(c)

Substituting Different Cymbal Patterns

For further practice, students can play all the 3.5a and 3.5b exercises substituting quarter or sixteenth notes for the hi-hat eighth notes. Exercise 3.5a3, for example, would be played like this:

Example 3.5a

Example 3.5b

Students should also practice moving the hi-hat pattern to the cymbal, which leaves the foot free to close the hi-hat on beats two and four.

Example 3.5c

Box 3.5b
ROCK DRUMMING: KEEPING TIME ON THE DRUM SET

WHAT TO WATCH FOR
- The hands stay out of each other's way when playing time on the hi-hat
- The bass drum pedal is lifted back off the drum after striking, not buried into the head

WHAT TO LISTEN FOR
- Steady tempos (especially at slower tempos)
- A clean attack when multiple instruments are struck at the same time
- A strong backbeat
- Controlled, even bass drum notes
- Balance and clarity among the instruments

Incorporating the Exercises
into Your Program

Have your students practice the previous exercises, and make them, and other exercises like them, a regular part of your testing schedule. There is no reason that, along with snare drum, mallet, and timpani techniques, drum set techniques should not be considered an essential part of your program.

CHAPTER 3.6

Solos and Fills

THE BACKGROUND

Whether drummers are called upon to play a two-bar fill or an eight-bar solo, key elements of the preparation are the same: they must practice improvising a given number of beats or bars that are rhythmic, musical, and secure.

The key word here is "improvising"—expressing music drawn from an internalized, musical vocabulary rather than from notes on a page. There are numerous ways to approach the art of solo improvisation.

An important resource for this vocabulary is recorded fills and solos played by leading instrumentalists both past and present. Whether the context is a rock band, jazz trio, or big band, students must take their cues from the masters and work out and expand upon similar patterns in the practice room.

Other sources of vocabulary, presented later, can come from various rhythmic patterns—exercises either found in books or made up by students on their own.

Orchestrating Patterns

Accented triplet or eighth-note patterns are a great resource for developing fills. They can sound fine played on the snare drum alone, but by experimenting with playing the accented notes on different tom-toms— "orchestrating" a pattern—students will develop fluidity around the drum set. At the same time, this kind of experimentation opens the door to a wealth of creative possibilities as students discover how to create patterns of greater interest and complexity.

Students can also create and orchestrate their own rhythmic patterns, accented or not, which can start from something as simple as a bar of eighth notes.

In band charts, short fills are often written out in the drum part. While I suggest that beginning students learn to play the written solo/fill to clarify and internalize its shape and length, in general, written fills, like the drum parts themselves, are meant to be guidelines.

It's important to convey to your students that a fill or solo need not be technically difficult to sound good. Playing a few well-placed notes *musically* serves the music far better than trying to impress with lots of notes that are rhythmically and technically insecure. More often than not, playing less is just what is needed.

TEACHING THE FUNDAMENTALS
Orchestrating Accents around the Drums

Exercise 3.6a An accented pattern on snare drum (eighth-note triplets).

Exercise 3.6b Orchestration #1.

Exercise 3.6c Orchestration #2.

After practicing Exercise 3.6a, students can try orchestrating the accents on various combinations of drums as shown in Exercises 3.6b and 3.6c. The classic Ted Reed book *Syncopation* is an excellent resource for material that can be used for orchestration.

Compressing Time

Exercise 3.6d Compressing the accent patterns around the set.

Exercise 3.6e Orchestration #1.

Exercise 3.6f Orchestration #2.

When it comes to playing triplet fills and solos, eighth-note triplets flow very easily from the triplet-based jazz ride rhythm (see chapter 3.3, Box 3.3f, *Jazz Drumming*, page 97). By compressing the eighth-note triplet patterns in Exercises 3.6a through 3.6c into sixteenth-note patterns, the triplets fit neatly into the eighth-note pulse found in rock and Latin drumming.

Note that students will have to be aware of the placement of bass drum and hi-hat notes as they switch from eighth-note to sixteenth-note patterns.

Transitioning from Timekeeping to Playing a Fill and Back

Exercise 3.6g Transition: jazz ride to fill.

Exercise 3.6h Transition: rock beat to fill.

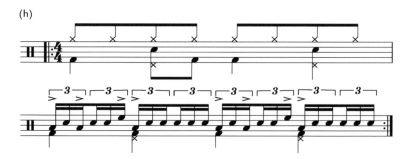

To develop their sense of time and the ability to transition into fills more smoothly, students should practice leading into the fill after a bar or several bars of timekeeping. Students can practice playing four-bar phrases by playing two bars of time followed by two bars of fill or three bars of time followed by one bar of fill.

Note that the jazz ride cymbal rhythm illustrated in Exercise 3.6g is missing the last note of the broken triplet on beat four. Leaving it out allows the drummer to comfortably begin the fill with the right hand.

Orchestrating Rhythmic Phrases

Exercise 3.6i Rhythmic phrase on snare and bass drum.

Exercise 3.6j Orchestration #1.

Exercise 3.6k Orchestration #2.

Any rhythmic phrase, from the most simple to the most complex, can be orchestrated. Exercise 3.6i becomes increasingly complex as the original snare drum phrase morphs into two new phrases played over the drum set. Notice how in Exercises 3.6j and 3.6k, the bass drum is included in the solo line. For added interest, the hi-hat can be added on beats two and four. Students can work with any number of possibilities, developing ideas as complex as their technique, musical knowledge, and imagination will allow.

PART 4

The Mallet Instruments

Introduction

The Mallet Instruments

It's likely that most students entering a junior high school music program have never *seen* a mallet instrument played before—other than, perhaps, in a marching band—and I'd wager that most percussionists *finish* high school having never seen and heard a vibraphonist, xylophonist, or marimbist on a concert stage, bandstand, or in a jazz club. With no role models to fuel their imaginations or inspire them, should we be surprised if we find many students unenthusiastic when it comes to playing mallets?

When students choose to play percussion, the last thing on their minds is struggling to sight-read music on orchestra bells. They may be curious about the instrument at first, but all too often interest wanes over time.

If you intend to have your percussionists play mallet instruments—which I recommend for a number of reasons (see later)—be sure to make that clear from the outset. Then, as time goes on, introduce your students to great performers and performances on the instruments: soloists performing on marimba and vibraphone; percussionists playing band and orchestral music that features mallet instruments; and great jazz musicians playing vibraphone and even marimba. (See companion website ⏵ for links to performances on mallet instruments.)

If, for whatever reason, an instrumental program does not include mallet instruments (see chapter 1.2, *Planning Your Percussion Program*), a band member who plays piano might be able to cover a not-too-difficult part when needed. But let's look at a few reasons your percussionists should be required to have a technical facility and understanding of keyboard instruments.

THE CASE FOR MALLET INSTRUMENTS
IN YOUR PROGRAM

First of all—and this is especially true throughout the early stages of playing—performing mallet exercises from the method book in addition to the snare exercises provides your percussionists with more to play while the rest of the class struggles with fingerings, intonation, and reading. Playing nothing other than quarter notes on a snare drum for a few weeks can be a bit of a snooze. (See chapter 1.3, *Challenging the Beginning Percussionist.*)

Second, the study of keyboard instruments provides your percussionists with a context for the understanding of theory. Drummers without a melodic instrument as a reference point won't relate to what you're talking about when you teach the staff—let alone keys, scales, or intervals—and they will undoubtedly tune out if what you're teaching has no connection to their instrument.

Finally, though not least of all, the impact of many of the scores you'll want to play will be diminished without the unique colors that mallet instruments provide.

ACCESSING THE INSTRUMENTS FOR PRACTICE

A major challenge facing percussionists is their limited access to the mallet instruments. Other than the bells, mallet instruments are not very portable and can't be taken home. Practice times are limited to lunch periods, recess, or before or after school. Some schools encourage bells to be taken home—one school I know had each percussionist rent a set for the year. But while students can improve note recognition and acquire a few basic skills by practicing on bells, they are not really a satisfactory instrument with which to develop one's technique. Aside from the bars being too small, their uncontrollable ringing can, over a practice session, become pretty annoying (make sure you have rubber mallets rather than hard plastic ones available for practice purposes). For more advanced pieces, the range might be limited too.

Perhaps the best compromise is for students to have a weekly practice session scheduled in the music room on a larger instrument, along with a set of bells available to sign out and take home.

Whatever the arrangement, make sure your students clearly understand the requirements of your program—and then see to it that *all* your percussionists rotate through *all* the instruments each and every music period.

THE MALLET INSTRUMENTS

Note: While instruments with greater and smaller ranges are also produced, the ranges of the instruments listed in this section are those most commonly found on school instruments.

Xylophone

- Range: 3-1/2 octaves, starting from the written F below middle C
- Sounds one octave higher than written

The best xylophones have rosewood bars. Less expensive practice instruments may have padauk bars. The bars of school models are often synthetic. Xylophone have a brighter, more brittle sound than marimbas.

Marimba

- Range: 4-1/3 octaves, starting from the written A one-and-a-third octaves below middle C
- Sounds as written
- The best instruments have rosewood bars. Less expensive practice instruments may have padauk bars. The bars of school models are often synthetic. Marimbas have a warmer, more resonant sound than xylophones.

Vibraphone

- Range: 3 octaves, starting from the written F below middle C
- Sounds as written

Vibraphone bars are made of a metal alloy. Like a piano, they have a foot pedal to control sustain. The vibraphone, through fans underneath the bars that are driven by a variable-speed motor, can electronically create a vibrato effect.

Glockenspiel (Orchestra Bells)

- Range: 2-1/2 octaves, starting from the written G or F below middle C
- Sounds two octaves higher than written
- The bars are made of metal.

Box 4.1a
MALLET INSTRUMENTS AND RELATED EQUIPMENT

- Kelon xylophones and marimbas: These instruments don't match the tonal quality of good wooden instruments, but their superior durability gives them a considerable advantage in a classroom setting.
- Vibraphones and marimbas with graduated bars: Professional instruments have bars that get progressively wider from the top to the bottom of the instrument. They produce a warmer, bigger sound than those with nongraduated bars, but cost more money. If you're on a tighter budget, the major companies make good-quality instruments with nongraduated bars.

RECOMMENDED MALLETS

A number of fine manufacturers make mallets designed for the various instruments. Note that *two* pairs of mallets will be needed for four-mallet parts.

For Xylophone and Bells . . .
- Hard rubber mallets with rattan handles for general playing and for playing softer passages
- Plastic mallets with rattan handles for very bright passages

Make sure that hard plastic mallets are reserved exclusively for the bells and xylophone, but even then, watch how they impact on your xylophone. Instruments of inferior wood could end up dented and, ultimately, out of tune.

Brass mallets are also available for bells. Avoid them, or at least use them cautiously. Unless your bells are of a very high quality, brass mallets can leave dents on the bars.

For Marimba and Vibraphone . . .
- Yarn mallets with rattan handles

Yarn mallets come in various degrees of hardness. There are many vibraphone and marimba mallets available. If they're too soft, you don't hear the attack, especially in the instruments' upper registers; too hard and you hear too much of a bang on impact, especially in the lower registers. It's difficult to audition keyboard mallets; stores that have a few pairs don't often have instruments to test them on. You'll likely have to rely on the manufacturer's description and/or a knowledgeable salesperson. Some manufacturers' sites provide audio samples demonstrating the sound quality of different mallets.

CHAPTER 4.2

Holding the Mallets

The Two- and Four-Mallet Grips

THE BACKGROUND

The vast majority of high school band mallet parts are written for two mallets. Nevertheless, some advanced-level pieces do call for the playing of three- or four-note chords and the execution of single lines while holding four mallets. Increasingly, more advanced percussionists have to acquire a basic facility with four-mallet technique.

There are three commonly used four-mallet grips. Each of them has advantages and disadvantages (Box 4.2a,), and they all have practitioners who perform complex solo literature at the highest technical level.

I have chosen to outline here the Burton grip. It is the grip I use, and one that is widely used by jazz vibraphonists, as well as a grip that is increasingly adopted by concert marimbists as well.

Note that playing with four mallets is not a progression from playing with two. The techniques are not related, and students who show interest should not be discouraged to dive right in to four-mallet playing from the beginning.

Indeed, while most students will likely be satisfied achieving sufficient control over four mallets to simply play the band parts, their four-mallet studies need not end there. With an ever-growing catalog of four-mallet repertoire available at all performance levels, students can be encouraged to learn a variety of pieces for independent study, for classroom performance, and/or for evaluation.

TEACHING THE FUNDAMENTALS
The Two-Mallet Grip

Illustration 4.2a shows the two-mallet grip, which is very similar to the matched grip on snare drum. It should not present a great problem for your students.

Illustration 4.2a The two-mallet grip, with the hands flat and close to the keyboard.

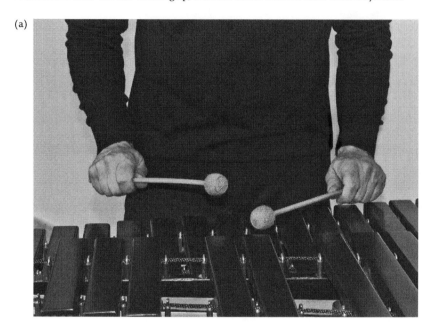

Like the snare grip, the mallet is held firmly, but not tightly, between the thumb and index finger, about one-third of the way from the end of the shaft. The remaining fingers wrap around the handle of the mallet, keeping the handle in contact with the palm of the hand at all times. Unlike the snare grip, I would recommend that the pinky also curve up and remain in contact with the stick. When the stick is lifted, watch that the fingers don't flip out.

The hands should be flat and positioned close to the instrument—about 2 to 3 inches above the bars.

The Four-Mallet Grip

The Burton grip, developed by famed jazz vibraphonist Gary Burton, began to receive widespread interest in the 1960s. It provides the player with a good deal of power, and students adopting this grip should be able to achieve basic control over the four mallets with relative ease.

Holding Four Mallets

Most books number the mallets from 1 to 4 moving from left to right (Illustration 4.2b). This is the system I will use here, but note that some authors reverse the order of the numbers.

With the Burton grip, as opposed to the Stevens grip, further discussed in Box 4.2a, *Two More Four-Mallet Grips*, the mallets in each hand cross under the palm, with the outside mallets 1 and 4 crossing on top of the inside mallets 2 and 3 (Illustration 4.2c).

Illustration 4.2b The numbered mallets.

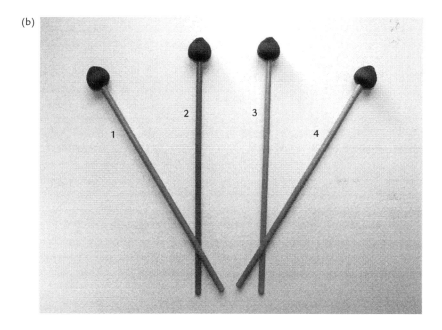

Illustration 4.2c The Burton grip.

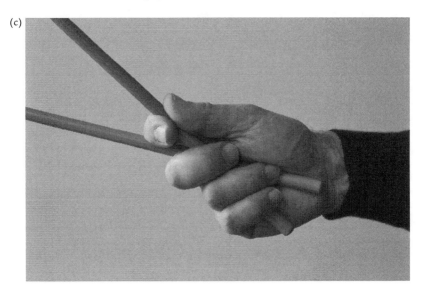

To further explain the grip, we begin with the right-hand placement of mallet 3, which is grasped like a single mallet, between the thumb and index finger. Mallet 4 is then inserted between the index and third fingers. It crosses above mallet 3.

The third and fourth fingers keep the mallets in place where they cross under the palm. For greater stability, I keep the fourth finger curled around the inside mallet—mallet 3 in the right hand—with the fingertip pressed against the outside mallet.

To hold the mallets in the left hand, follow the previous directions, substituting mallet 2 for mallet 3 and mallet 1 for mallet 4.

Spreading and Closing Four Mallets

To play different intervals, the mallets are spread and closed using the fingers.

To practice this, we begin by holding the mallets of each hand at a 90-degree angle. In this position, both the thumbs and index fingers rest between the two mallets, with the thumbs curved down and over the tops of the inside mallets (Illustration 4.2d).

To close the spread, the fourth and fifth fingers of each hand push the bottom ends of mallets 2 and 3, moving the heads closer together. The index fingers begin to extend as the thumbs move to the outer side of mallets 2 and 3 to help push them in and further close the gap. To pull the mallets together as close as possible, the index fingers must finally be lifted up and above them (Illustration 4.2e).

Illustration 4.2d The mallets spread about 90 degrees.

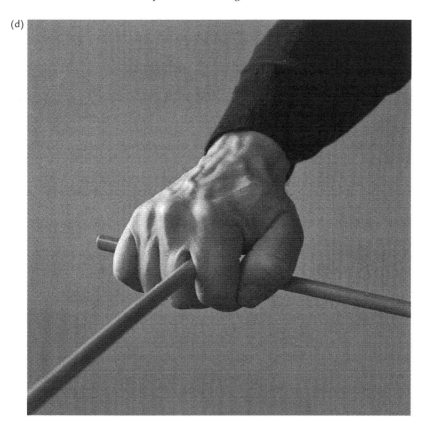

To spread the mallets apart, the index fingers move back between them, pushing the inside mallets away from the outer mallets, while the fourth and fifth fingers pull the mallets up from the bottom end. The thumbs shift back to their position between the two mallets to help move them back to their original 90-degree-angle spread.

Students should practice this exercise away from the keyboard—and gain a degree of comfort with its execution—before being required to play block intervals and chords on an instrument.

Illustration 4.2e The mallets pulled together as close as possible.

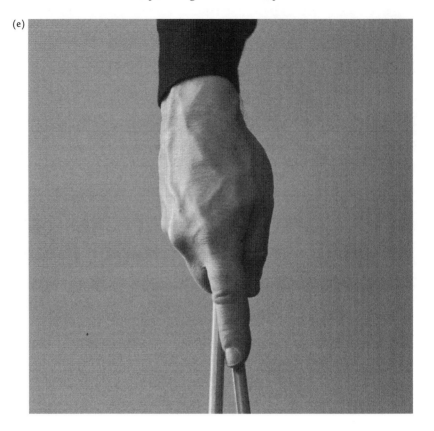

(e)

Box 4.2a

TWO MORE FOUR-MALLET GRIPS

Other than the Burton grip, outlined previously, the two most common four-mallet grips are the traditional grip, and the Stevens grip, developed by marimbist Leigh Howard Stevens. All are widely used and should definitely be considered by the student who plans a more in-depth study of concert or jazz mallet playing.

The traditional grip is related to the Burton grip in that (1) the sticks cross under the palm, and (2) the outer mallet is set between the index and third fingers. Where the two approaches differ is that with the Burton grip, the inner mallets cross below the outer mallets, while with the traditional grip, these positions are reversed. As well, with the Burton grip, single lines are played with mallets 2 and 4, while with the traditional grip, they are played with mallets 2 and 3.

The Stevens grip is quite different. Like the Burton and traditional grips, the thumb and index finger hold the inside mallet, but the outside mallet is set between the third and fourth fingers and is held with the fourth and fifth fingers curled around it, so two fingers separate the mallets rather than one. As a result, the sticks do not cross under the palm and are held more parallel to each other.

It would be difficult to say that any one of the three grips outlined here is necessarily better for a particular instrument. While Stevens is a classical marimbist and Burton is a jazz vibraphonist, great vibists can be found using variations of the Stevens grip and great marimbists often play with the Burton grip. (While not too many jazz vibists use the traditional grip, it is still widely used by orchestral percussionists.) Students—of jazz in particular—should consider how the different grips may lend themselves to different musical approaches to the instrument.

Advantages of the Stevens grip are that it allows for wider-interval spreads and lends itself to more independent control over each stick. The Burton grip, on the other hand, offers greater power and the ability to change intervals quickly. While the traditional grip falls somewhere between those two, it's important to keep in mind that successful exponents of *any* of the grips outlined here are able to convincingly overcome their shortcomings.

The bottom line is that all three grips have advantages and disadvantages, and beginning mallet players should explore them further and watch videos of the great classical and jazz mallet players to see which grip appeals to them most.

Playing Mallet Instruments

THE BACKGROUND

The information in this chapter applies to mallet playing in general, no matter what the grip or instrument, unless specifically noted.

While the exercises included here can be practiced on all mallet instruments, practicing on bells is not as satisfying as on xylophone, marimba, or vibraphone. In general, the exercises are more difficult to execute on bells; the smaller bars necessitate that the mallet heads be held closer together, and it's more of a challenge to keep them out of each other's way. That being said, any practicing on the bells is better than not practicing at all.

TEACHING THE FUNDAMENTALS
Positioning the Body: Marimba and Xylophone

When playing mallet instruments other than the vibraphone, students should stand with their feet spread comfortably about a foot apart. They should position themselves in the middle of the range of notes they will be playing.

On marimba or xylophone, whenever possible, students should shift their weight onto the right or left leg as they play up or down the instrument, swaying the body from side to side parallel to the keyboard. When playing over wider ranges on larger instruments, it will be necessary to step to the right or left, keeping their bodies parallel to the instrument.

Note that if the body twists from the waist rather than remaining parallel to the instrument when moving up and down the keyboard, the position of the wrists change. This changes the position of the heads of the mallets over the bars. A twist from the waist is necessary only when making wide leaps up or down the instrument.

Positioning the Body: The Vibraphone and Pedaling

When playing vibraphone, the right foot stays in position on the pedal. With the range usually limited to three octaves (some companies are manufacturing instruments with an extended lower range), the left foot need not move. By leaning slightly from side to side, percussionists will find that all the notes of the instrument are easily within reach.

With the heel kept on the floor, the pedal is manipulated with the top part of the foot. Pressing the pedal all the way down to the floor is not necessary and creates noise. Pressing down lightly on the pedal is enough to disengage the felt from the bars and allow them to ring.

Vibraphone music will often notate pedaling, but not always. Percussionists/vibraphonists must often use their own musical discretion as to how much pedal to use, and to what extent notes should be allowed to ring together.

Where to Strike the Bar

The "white" notes of mallet instruments are always played in the area between the two nodes—the points where the string runs through the bars. Playing directly on the node produces a thin sound and must be avoided.

Striking the middle of the "black" bars, however, is not always convenient. It's often much easier to hit the section below the nodes on the "black" bars— the section that, on xylophone and marimba, extends over the "white" notes, and that on vibraphone rests on the felt damper. When striking the middle of the "black" bar is too difficult—when playing quick scale passages, for example—striking the lower section of the bar presents no problem at all.

Hand Position: Playing with Two Mallets

In general, the mallets are held directly in front of the center of the student's body, angled from one another and forming a "V" shape. The head of the left-hand mallet is placed ahead of that in the right hand, as shown in Illustration 4.3a, a position that helps prevent the mallets from colliding together.

Illustration 4.3a The mallets form a "V" shape, with the left mallet placed ahead of the right.

(a)

As reading is notoriously difficult on mallet instruments (see chapter 4.4, *Sight-Reading on Mallet Instruments*), it's important that the mallet player, unable to *see* where the heads of the mallets are, be able to *sense* where they are. For this reason, the mallets should be kept in the same position relative to the body as much as possible, allowing the student to read and play with greater accuracy.

To maintain the mallets in a consistent position in relation to the body, keep two points in mind:

- The body stays parallel to the instrument as much as possible.
- The hands remain flat, palms facing down, not turned to a thumbs-on-top position.

Note that moving the wrists from a flat position, with the thumbs at the sides of the mallets, to a position with the thumbs up, shifts the mallet heads to different positions over the instrument, as discussed in Box 4.3a, *Hands On: Demonstrating Why the Wrists Should Stay Flat.*

Box 4.3a

HANDS-ON: DEMONSTRATING WHY THE WRISTS SHOULD STAY FLAT

Have your student stand at the instrument. The mallets should be in the "V" position over two neighboring notes, with the hands close to the bars. Make sure the wrists are flat, with the thumbs at the side. Point out that this is the default hand position, the one in which it should remain as much as possible.

To demonstrate what happens when this position is changed, have the student slowly turn the wrists so that the thumbs are on top of the mallet shaft. Note that the heads of the mallets move to the right and left, and end up positioned above two different notes. If the hands are regularly moving from the thumbs at the side to the thumbs-on-top position, it is much more difficult to play and sight-read accurately.

The Stroke

As with the snare drum, students should not hammer the mallet down into the instrument; it should be *dropped* down and lifted up off the bar with a wrist movement.

To play evenly, the mallets must be lifted and dropped from the same height.

Hand Position: Playing with Four Mallets

Illustration 4.3b shows how, with the Burton grip (see chapter 4.2, pages 129–131), single-note passages are generally played with mallets 2 and 4. Mallets 1 and 3 should not move up and down. They rotate, serving as pivot points while the other mallets—their heads moving in an arc-like shape— are lifted and dropped.

To help students get the feel of playing single strokes in the right hand, have them spread the mallets to roughly an 80-degree angle with mallet 4 pointing straight out from the hand. Then form a kind of ball and socket with the head of mallet 3 held loosely with the fingers of either your hand or the student's free hand. Mallet 4 should now be lifted and dropped as mallet 3 rotates within the socket *without* moving up and down.

The motion with the left hand is different from that of the right. The mallets should be spread to roughly a 45-degree angle, with mallet 1

Illustration 4.3b The Burton grip: Playing single notes with mallets 2 and 4.

pointing straight out from the hand. We now create the ball and socket with the head of mallet 1 to prevent it from moving up and down while students lift and drop mallet 2 by rotating the wrist.

Scalar Exercises

The exercises in this section can be assigned as soon as your students start working on scales. They can be transposed to whatever scale is being studied and, depending on the tempo at which they are played, will provide technical challenges for students at any level.

If students are studying four-mallet techniques, they should practice any single-note exercises with the appropriate two mallets.

Exercise 4.3a Sixteenth notes on each scale degree.

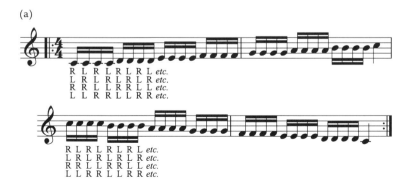

Students should practice Exercise 4.3a, and other similar exercises, using different stickings to develop dexterity. When double stroking the sixteenth notes, they must play the second stroke with a distinct wrist movement and listen for a note that has as much weight and volume as the first.

Exercise 4.3b Eighth-note scale pattern.

Exercise 4.3c Eighth-note triplet scale pattern.

When exercises such as 4.3b and 4.3c are played on mallet instruments, patterns should be practiced starting on both the right and left hand. Note the double sticking patterns. They are commonly used to avoid stickings that would otherwise be awkward to play. Students should listen for the more legato phrasing that double stickings produce.

Rolling on Xylophone and Marimba

Exercise 4.3d Rolling on each scale degree.

(d)

Note: "R" or "L" denotes the hand starting the roll

Exercise 4.3e Ending a roll on a different scale degree.

(e)

Rolls on xylophone or marimba are played faster or slower depending on the pitch of the note, and are always played with single strokes. As with timpani, higher-pitched notes, with shorter wavelengths, are rolled faster than lower-pitched notes that have longer wavelengths. The need to vary the speed of the roll is more pronounced on marimba, given the contrast between its lower, more resonant register and dry upper register. Vibraphone notes are usually sustained by pedaling rather than by rolling.

The challenge of these exercises is playing an even roll at an appropriate speed—which can be quite quick, especially in the higher register—then landing on the following note *exactly* on the beat. For this reason, they should ideally be practiced with a metronome at various tempos.

Note: Students should avoid initiating each roll with an accent!

Exercises for Four Mallets

Exercise 4.3f Four mallets: widening the interval keeping mallets 1 and 3 stationary.

(f)

1) Played right hand alone with mallets 3 and 4
2) Played left hand alone with mallets 1 and 2

Exercise 4.3g Four mallets: widening the interval keeping mallets 2 and 4 stationary.

1) Played right hand alone with mallets 3 and 4
2) Played left hand alone with mallets 1 and 2

For each hand to gain control playing intervals, students should practice spreading and closing the mallets in each hand while *away* from the instrument (see chapter 4.2, *Spreading and Closing Four Mallets*, pages 130–132). Once comfortable doing that, they should practice manipulating the mallets to play intervals at the keyboard as shown in Exercises 4.3f and 4.3g.

Exercise 4.3h Playing broken chords with four mallets.

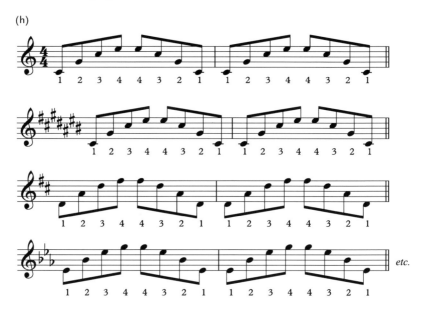

With mallets 2 and 4 used to play single lines, it's easy to neglect the importance of developing power and accuracy with mallets 1 and 3. Aside from broken chord exercises such as Exercise 4.3h, students can play any scale written for two mallets (Exercises 4.3b or 4.3c, for example) with any of the four mallets alone.

Box 4.3b

PLAYING MALLET INSTRUMENTS

WHAT TO WATCH FOR

- Mallets forming a "V" shape
- Left mallet placed ahead of the right mallet
- Lifting and dropping the mallet from the wrist
- Lifting and dropping the mallet from the same height
- Avoiding the nodes when striking the bar
- Keeping the body parallel to the keyboard

WHAT TO LISTEN FOR

- Even volume from both mallets when playing scalar lines
- Rolls played at appropriate speeds

The "B-Flat" Scale: Crossing the Mallets

The scale that every band class starts out playing, the "B-flat" scale, can cause some difficulty for the beginning mallet student. It's a problem that comes up when playing a number of other scales too, so it is best to deal with it right off the bat.

When starting the "B-flat" scale with the left hand moving from the "B-flat" to "D," the right hand, moving from the "C" to the "E-flat," has difficulty getting out of its way. Students tend to make an awkward U-shaped movement with the right mallet—swinging it too far to the right before bringing it back in to hit the "E-flat"—thinking that that's the only means of avoiding a collision.

In fact, all they have to do is get that right mallet off the C *as soon as possible* and move it *in a straight line* up to the E-flat. If they hesitate too long on the C, the mallets will indeed collide.

Avoiding *any* superfluous motion when playing will lead to a better technique, as well as more accurate sight-reading.

Sight-Reading on Mallet Instruments

THE BACKGROUND

When it comes to sight-reading, no instrument poses a greater challenge than a mallet instrument.

Brass and wind players, with their instruments' valves or keys at their fingertips, readily sight-read without ever having to take their eyes off the music. Percussionists, on the other hand, have no direct physical contact with the mallet instrument they are playing. They are expected to focus on music perched on a stand above and beyond the keyboard in front of them and then maneuver mallets—completely separating them from the instrument—like precision-guided missiles seeking bars laid out *somewhere* below them and out of sight.

Beginning mallet players find it next to impossible to keep their eyes on the music, and as the parts become more difficult, they become increasingly frustrated having to memorize them just to keep up with the rest of the class. Ultimately, they often give up on mallets altogether.

But there are a few steps your students can take that will lead to better reading on mallet instruments (and leave you with at least one musician to play those vibe or xylophone parts that add so much color to the score).

TEACHING THE FUNDAMENTALS
Peripheral Vision and Positioning the Music

To sight-read well on mallet instruments, it is important that the music stand, as seen in Illustration 4.4a, be placed so that the instrumentalist can see the keyboard using peripheral vision.

Your students must first determine the range of their part, then place their stand in the middle of that range. If the xylophone part goes from a "middle C" to the "G" a perfect fifth above, the stand should be centered in front of the "E." If the range extends from the "middle C" to the "G" an octave-and-a-half higher, the music should be centered more or less in front of the "A" or "B" above "middle C."

Illustration 4.4a Music stand placement for reading on mallet instruments.

With the stand in the right place, it should be lowered so that the bottom of the desk is just above the keyboard and turned outward. The music is now in the optimal position to be read using peripheral vision.

Have your students play parts slowly. If they keep their eyes on the music, they will still be able to see the far ends of the "black" keys, and from there gauge where the other notes are.

Keep in mind that there are certain intervallic leaps that would challenge even the most seasoned professional, and there are times, particularly when playing on instruments with larger keyboards, when it's okay to look down.

The Importance of Hand Position

To read with any accuracy on mallet instruments, the points on hand position discussed in chapter 4.3, *Hand Position: Playing with Two Mallets*, pages 136–138, must become second nature.

The percussionist, unable to see the head of the mallet when sight-reading, must nevertheless know where it is. Using peripheral vision to locate the keys is only half the battle. Your percussionists must remember the points covered earlier to sense where the head of the mallet is:

- When playing up or down the keyboard, the body weight shifts from one leg to the other as the student leans from side to side. The body does not twist from the hip.
- Keep the hands flat, with the thumb at the side of the mallet.
- The mallets form a "V" shape.

If percussionists don't have a clear sense of where the head of the mallet is, they will forever have difficulty playing accurately, adding another level of insecurity to the already difficult task of sight-reading.

CHAPTER 4.5

Evaluating Mallet Instrument Performance

As with snare drum, keep in mind that the performance challenges for the mallet player are generally not at all similar to those for the woodwind or brass player.

An example of this is the student who rushed in to see me at the last minute before having to play his "B-flat" scale test. He had never taken a mallet lesson, had not prepared for the test at all, and hadn't a clue as to which notes to hit. Immediately after I pointed out the notes of the scale to him, he grabbed the mallets and, summoning no particular technique, banged them out at a moderate tempo.

No doubt he did well on the test. Ultimately, of course, he learned nothing and got away with murder.

No practice is necessary to play a note on a xylophone. Playing simple passages on any mallet instrument is a piece of cake for the percussionist, and with minimal effort, anyone can memorize a short passage and play all the notes necessary to ace a play test.

Again, as with snare drum—and especially at the beginning of the first year—you might consider adding one or more of the following into the framework of your tests:

- Require that the test be played at an appropriately quick tempo, at an assigned metronome marking.
- Require that the test be played at a very slow tempo (a great exercise to develop a good sense of time; students don't realize how difficult this can be).

• Reserve a portion of your mark for form (mallets form a "V" shape and move straight up and down; thumbs at the sides; left mallet positioned above the right mallet on the bar, etc.).

If you remain aware of what challenges your percussionists and what doesn't, it won't take a lot of extra effort to ensure they play tests that demand thought and preparation.

PART 5

The Timpani

Introduction

The Timpani

Ideally, a percussion program would require the study of timpani. Students would, through the years, improve their bass clef reading skills and interval recognition, and would graduate from playing two drums to playing four as they improve their ability to tune and retune drums throughout the performance of a piece. It's a tall order—especially when you take into account that they are also responsible for learning snare drum, drum set, and xylophone. It's one more challenging instrument, and in real life, all but the most serious students might be overwhelmed—if not discouraged—when faced with having to learn timpani. This is a pity, because timpani are a lot of fun to play. The late David Searcy, timpanist with the La Scala Orchestra, vividly described them as the orchestra's "nerve center," and playing timpani can make for a thrilling experience. Nevertheless, in high schools, scratched and dented drums are more often used as tabletops than for the production of the spectacular sounds they are capable of.

WHY YOU SHOULD INCLUDE TIMPANI IN YOUR PROGRAM

First, the reasons I can think of for *not* including timpani in your percussion course are that (1) they cost a lot of money, (2) they take up a lot of space, and (3) they are not easily accessible for practicing.

But if you have the budget and space for timpani, providing your students with at least a basic understanding of performance technique is a good idea. Like mallet instruments, they provide music to play when a score is light on other percussion. They are also the only percussion instrument that requires your students to consider intonation—an aspect of music that all your other instrumentalists must deal with. Finally, it goes without saying that timpani parts are sorely missed when left out of a score.

So it's a good idea for your percussionists to at least get their feet wet playing timpani. And who knows—maybe being the "nerve center" of the orchestra is just what one of your students needs to ignite his or her musical passion.

THE TIMPANI RANGES

While it is difficult to give a precise tuning range for each drum size, the following numbers provide reasonable guidelines to follow:

32-inch drum: D to A
29-inch drum: F to C
26-inch drum: B-flat to F
23-inch drum: D to A

Box 5.1a

TIMPANI AND RELATED EQUIPMENT

Timpani sizes, in order of importance, are

- 26 inch and 29 inch, then 32 inch, then 23 inch.

Copper bowls produce a better tone than fiberglass bowls, but cost more. You likely won't be disappointed with fiberglass timpani—they sound good and are a good choice if the budget is tight.

Get good covers—and make sure they are always on when the timpani are not being played.

RECOMMENDED MALLETS

- A general purpose pair
- A pair with heavier, softer heads for lower notes
- A hard pair for playing staccato and achieving greater definition on high notes and quieter passages

Playing Timpani

THE BACKGROUND
Positioning the Timpani

Timpani in North America are traditionally arranged with the lowest drum to the left. In several European countries—primarily Germany, Austria, and Holland—they are traditionally arranged with the lowest drum to the right.

Tuning

The best way to tune timpani is by ear. Professionals—with the aid of a tuning fork pitched at whatever "A" the orchestra tunes to—will hear the required pitch in their head, quietly strike the drum, then pedal to the target note. Good timpanists must have good relative pitch and the ability to recognize, sing, and match intervals—often while counting bars with the ensemble playing very loudly! It can be extremely difficult but is a skill that anyone seriously considering a future playing percussion must develop.

Expecting the majority of percussion students to rely on their ear exclusively for tuning would be excessive, and I recommend that, in general, they use the gauges, especially when tuning within a movement. But keep in mind that the gauges are not precise, so work with your students on fine-tuning by ear when possible—certainly at the beginning of each piece and its subsequent movements. Make sure too that the gauges are checked regularly for accuracy.

Whether tuning by ear or with gauges, the target pitch must be approached from below.

When tuning a drum by ear, the head is struck lightly with the mallet or the tip of the middle finger. If the target pitch is *above* the struck note, the pedal is slowly pushed down to raise the note. A quiet glissando is heard as the pitch slides into that of the target note. If the target pitch is *below* the struck note, the drum must first be tuned down to a pitch below the target note before being raised to the correct pitch. The pitch is then checked with another quiet tap.

When tuning the drum with gauges, the student need not hit the drum at the beginning of the process. Depending on the student's playing level, he or she might tap the drum at the end of the tuning to check the pitch.

To change pitches within a movement, timpanists will often write the notes' letter names in pencil onto the part. If an "F" on the 32-inch drum must be tuned to a "G" four bars later, the timpanist would write "F to G" above the staff just after the last "F." If three or more timpani are being played, it may be helpful to assign numbers to the drums and write them next to the corresponding note change. For example, if both the 26- and 32-inch drums must be tuned, and the drums are numbered 1 to 4 from high to low, we could write "2 - C to D" just above "4 – F to G."

TEACHING THE FUNDAMENTALS
Positioning the Body

Playing a set of two or four timpani, the timpanist stands in the center of the group of drums, facing the conductor. With both feet planted firmly on the ground, the timpanist rotates the upper body as necessary when moving from drum to drum.

The Grip

There are two common grips for the timpani mallet.

Playing with the German grip, the wrists are flat, the thumbs are placed at the side of the stick, and the mallets form a "V" at almost a 90-degree angle.

Playing with the French grip, the wrists are turned inward, the thumbs rest on top of the stick, and the mallets are more or less parallel to each other.

I'm most comfortable playing somewhere in between, with the wrists angled mid-way between the German and French positions, and the sticks placed in a moderately angled "V" shape (Illustration 5.2a).

Illustration 5.2a Playing position and timpani mallet grip.

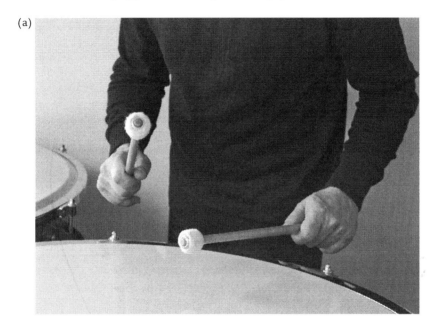

With the thumb and index fingers opposite each other, fingers three and four curl under the mallet for support. The fifth finger drops slightly away.

The Stroke

The problem with most timpani playing at the high school level is that beginning percussionists beat down into the drum (a method that's not recommend for snare drumming either) and produce a "bang" rather than a full, warm tone.

Exercise 5.2a Playing even quarter notes.

Exercise 5.2b Playing even eighth and quarter notes over two timpani.

(b)

Your timpanists should be trying to achieve as even a sound as possible on the drums.

As with all percussion, a relaxed and unforced stroke is important. Tension in the arm, wrist, and fingers is to be avoided at all times. Louder notes are played by letting the stick and forearm *fall* into the drum from a higher level. As mentioned earlier, *it is important that your percussionists do not hammer the mallet into the timpani.*

Once the head is struck, *the mallet is lifted off immediately,* with the upstroke following the natural rebound off the head. The downstroke and upstroke should be one fluid motion—with the drop of the wrist leading smoothly into the upstroke. Watch too that the mallets move straight up and down.

Each drum is struck approximately 4 inches from the edge of the instrument. If timpani are played too close to the center, there is not enough tone; if they are played too close to the edge, the sound is thin.

Box 5.2a

STRIKING THE TIMPANI

WHAT TO WATCH FOR
- Arms relaxed at the student's sides
- A relaxed downstroke leading smoothly into an upstroke
- The mallet moving in a straight up-and-down motion
- The mallets dropping from, and returning to, the same height
- The mallets striking the drum about 4 inches from the edge
- Students turning slightly from the waist, without moving their feet, when moving from drum to drum

WHAT TO LISTEN FOR
- An even attack

Sticking Patterns

Timpanists use alternate sticking whenever possible to achieve the most consistent quality of sound and attack. However, doing so when playing patterns between timpani may lead to cross-sticking—crossing one hand/mallet over the other when moving between timpani—which can easily result in undesired accents and/or uneven tone quality.

Depending on the context, the need to cross-stick between timpani can be avoided by doing one of three things:

- Playing a double stroke (making sure that the second stroke is executed with a distinct wrist movement for clear articulation)
- Shifting both sticks in a lateral motion to the second drum if the tempo allows
- As shown in Exercises 5.2c through 5.2e, making sure the pattern played on the first drum is initiated by the appropriate hand

Cross-sticking is, nevertheless, an important and useful technique to learn when having to move quickly between drums, and the patterns shown in Exercises 5.2f and 5.2g should be practiced slowly and thoughtfully while carefully following the guidelines in Box 5.2b.

Box 5.2b

PLAYING CROSSOVER STROKES

WHAT TO WATCH FOR
- The crossover mallet makes as low and smooth an arc as possible
- The crossover mallet strikes the drums slightly beyond the point it would normally strike—to the right on a higher drum or to the left on a lower drum—before returning to its normal position.
- The mallet that crosses over strikes the same spot on the drum consistently

WHAT TO LISTEN FOR
- An unaccented crossover note
- Each note played with the same volume and quality of sound

Avoiding Crossover Strokes

Exercise 5.2c Avoiding crossover strokes playing eighth notes.

(c)

```
R  L  R     R  L  R     L  R  L     L  R  L
```

Exercise 5.2d Avoiding crossover strokes playing sixteenth notes.

(d)

Exercise 5.2e Avoiding crossover strokes playing triplets.

(e)

To play alternate stickings more consistently when moving between drums, even-numbered note patterns played on the first drum must be initiated with the inside hand, as shown in Exercises 5.2c and 5.2d.

Conversely, you must begin an odd-numbered note pattern with the outside hand, as shown in Exercise 5.2e.

Playing Crossover Strokes

Exercise 5.2f Crossing the right hand over the left.

(f)

Exercise 5.2g Crossing the left hand over the right.

(g)

There are times when a crossover stroke—an outer mallet crossing over an inner mallet to strike another drum—cannot be avoided. As it is generally more difficult to perform crossovers, alternate sticking is preferred.

At slower tempos, it is possible to play Exercises 5.2f and 5.2g without crossing one stick over the other. Using Exercise 5.2f as an example, both mallets can be shifted together in a lateral motion to the left and above the drum tuned to a "G" before striking.

At faster tempos, it may be impossible to avoid executing crossover strokes. As a result, students should practice crossovers slowly and carefully, watching that the sticks do not get in each other's way and that each timpani is struck consistently with an equal amount of force.

To play crossover strokes smoothly, the inside stick should still be in motion as the outer stick is crossing over and above it. The crossover stick makes a smooth arc to the upper or lower drum; moving from the "C" down to the "G" will require its landing *slightly* to the left of where it would normally strike the drum before returning to its normal position. Moving from the "G" to the "C" will require its landing slightly to the right of where it would normally strike the drum. The hands and arms should stay relaxed as the arc over the inside stick is kept as low as possible.

Rolling on Timpani

Rolls on timpani, except for the rare occasions they are specified otherwise, are always single stroked.

Generally speaking, the lower the drum is, the slower the roll. Rolling too quickly on a low note interferes with the naturally longer wavelength and produces a roll that is choppy. Conversely, rolling too slowly on a higher note allows the shorter wavelength to dissipate too much before the next tone is produced, resulting in a sound that is not sustained. The timpanist should be trying to create as solid and even a tone as possible with the fewest number of strokes (though more experienced timpanists might play a faster roll if the desire is to create a sense of nervousness, for example).

Exercise 5.2h Rolling on different pitches.

Students should practice rolling on notes of different pitches. The strokes must be played at an even volume (remind your students that the sticks should be lifted to and dropped from a uniform height) and played at the most appropriate speed for the note.

Exercise 5.2i Rolls ending in a rest.

(i)

When a roll has an unarticulated ending, the mallets are simply lifted off the drum at the beginning of the rest. (Students should also practice dampening at the beginning of the rest, as explained in *Dampening/ Muffling the Timpani*, later.)

Exercise 5.2j Rolls ending in a note.

The connection from a roll to a single note must be seamless. Students must be sure to play the quarter note that ends the roll exactly on the beat.

Exercise 5.2k Rolls ending on a higher-pitched timpani.

Exercise 5.2l Rolls ending on a lower-pitched timpani.

When a roll ends on a different drum, it is not always clear which hand is going to be in the best position to play the final note. That uncertainty can lead to a lack of precision in its placement. Just remember that whatever the length of the roll—be it one beat, four beats, or four bars—the *last* beat before changing drums must consist of an even number of strokes if started with the inside hand and an odd number of strokes if started with the outside hand (see *Avoiding Crossover Strokes* earlier in this chapter).

Since the number of strokes required to play a roll depends on the pitch of the note and the tempo of the piece, Examples 5.2a and 5.2b illustrate rolls of differing speeds played over three beats. In each case, a single note is added to the roll one beat before changing drums, making the number of strokes odd or even as required, and resulting in a smooth movement to the final stroke.

Example 5.2a

(a)

Example 5.2b

(b)

Students should practice Exercises 5.2k and 5.2l using a metronome at different settings, focusing on the placement of that final note.

Rehearsing roll passages with your timpanists gives them the practice they need to play them at an appropriate pulse and end them with precision.

The Forte Piano Roll

A forte piano roll is begun by striking the drum with a single note at a forte level. The timpanist must listen as the note decays, and begin a roll to sustain the tone once the desired piano volume is reached.

The roll should be eased into gently, without any attack. If the *fp* roll is on a low note, the timpanist will wait longer before beginning the roll than if the note is on a higher-pitched drum with a shorter sustain. If the roll is on a very high-pitched drum, there will be no delay at all in beginning the roll.

Dampening/Muffling the Timpani

Dampening or muffling the timpani—stopping the instruments' ringing after a note is struck—is an important technique to be practiced. While a drum can often be dampened with the free hand, it is sometimes necessary that timpani be dampened by the same hand that plays the note.

To dampen timpani, the third, fourth, and fifth fingers fan out from their position under the stick. The top part of the fingers is placed on the drum head to diminish or completely stop the ringing. To dampen as silently as possible, the fingers are dropped onto the head from a position only slightly above it.

Exercise 5.2m Dampening the timpani.

(m)

Exercise 5.2m should be practiced the following ways:

- Striking all notes with the right hand and dampening with the left
- Striking all notes with the left hand and dampening with the right
- Striking and dampening the "C" with the right hand and the "G" with the left hand

Exercise 5.2n Dampening with one hand while striking another note.

(n)

X = dampen the preceding note

In Exercise 5.2n, the hand that strikes a note dampens it as well.

After playing the first note on the "C," the fingers of the right hand fan out and dampen the drum *exactly* at the moment the left mallet strikes the "G." The left hand then dampens the "G" at the moment the right hand strikes the "C."

PART 6

Bass Drum; Auxiliary Percussion

CHAPTER 6.1

Introduction

Bass Drum; Auxiliary Percussion

Snare drum, drum set, mallet instruments, and timpani are generally considered the core percussion instruments. Unfortunately, everything else is often taken much less seriously.

Though bass drum, and auxiliary instruments such as suspended and crash cymbals, tambourine, triangle and so forth, may not require the years of study and practice as those considered to be the cornerstones of percussion, there nevertheless *are* techniques to be learned, and music for these instruments can often be tricky.

That said, due to their relative simplicity, the performance of these instruments requires a particular mindset—a particularly *mature* mindset. They must be approached musically, and far too often, students don't put much thought or energy into their performance. Distractedly beating a bass drum on quarter notes does not amount to *playing* an instrument. Hitting a cymbal with whatever stick happens to be at hand rarely results in the most appropriate sound required for a particular score.

What students often don't appreciate is the important role of orchestral color in a score, and how the choice of instrument—a choice they should carefully and consciously make, particularly when it comes to cymbals and mallets—and the energy and musicality with which they play every single note make an enormous contribution to the success of the performance.

If you can get your students to understand the important role these instruments play in bringing music to life—how a persistent bass drum rhythm can perfectly underpin an unfolding drama, or how a carefully chosen cymbal or tambourine can make a piece sparkle—you will have gone a long way toward developing truly musical percussionists.

The Concert Bass Drum

STRIKING AND DAMPENING THE BASS DRUM

In general, the bass drum is struck slightly off the center of the head with a firm wrist stroke. When the drum is perpendicular—its position for the vast majority of playing—the amount of reverberation and length of the note are controlled by left-hand pressure against the resonant head (the head not struck by the mallet), right-knee pressure against the batter head, and, sometimes, right-hand pressure against the batter head.

Dampening with the Left Hand

In general playing, the percussionist holds the mallet in the right hand and leans into the instrument while placing the left hand in position over the resonant head. To produce a drier sound—necessary, for example, when playing a march requiring repeated quarter notes—the fingers of the left hand should touch the resonant head to cut the ring of the drum and allow for more clearly articulated quarter notes. The degree of pressure needed depends on a number of factors, such as the size of the drum, the tension on the head, the hardness of the mallet, the placement of the note on the drum (the closer to the center, the drier and more pointed the attack), and the volume of sound. The percussionist must be constantly listening and monitoring the sound produced, and respond accordingly.

Dampening with the Knee

To make passages even drier, or when playing notes that require sudden muffling, it is necessary to dampen with the knee and the left hand (Illustration 6.2a).

If your bass drum stand does not have a cross-bar that can be used as a foot rest, you must place a short stool or chair in front of the percussionist, to the right of the bass drum, to position the knee at an appropriate height for dampening.

Your percussionists can also use the knee in conjunction with the left hand to achieve clearer articulation. To do so, the knee should rest lightly on the batter head, while the left hand moves on and off the resonant head as necessary.

Illustration 6.2a Dampening the bass drum.

(a)

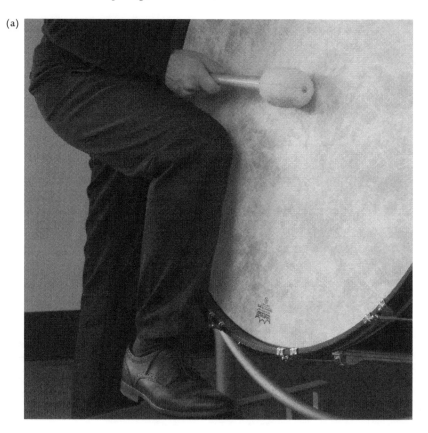

To suddenly and completely stop the drum's reverberation—for example, when a thunderous *double-forte* note is immediately followed by a *tutti* silence—the percussionist will have to dampen with the left hand and the knee together to fully stop the reverberation of a larger instrument.

BASS DRUM ROLLS

Rolls and quicker, articulated rhythmic passages may be played more easily on a tilted or flat bass drum.

Rolls are always single stroked. The mallets strike the head at points that are equidistant from its center. Avoiding playing at the center of the drum will result in less attack and a fuller, more resonant sound.

Note: Rolls and rhythmic passages are always played on the batter head of the drum only, never with one mallet striking the batter head and the other striking the resonant head.

When the drum cannot be tilted, students have to roll and play rhythmic passages with the left-hand mallet dropping down from the hand placed at the top of the drum. This is one time where traditional grip comes in handy: with the shaft of the stick resting between the thumb and the index finger, the index and third finger on top of the mallet, and the fourth finger underneath and supporting the mallet, the left-hand position is a lot less awkward.

If the student is unfamiliar with traditional grip, he or she can use matched grip, bending over sideways from the waist to play the roll.

PLAYING RHYTHMIC PASSAGES

Sometimes it's necessary to use both hands to play quick, rhythmic bass drum passages. As with the roll, they are most easily played with the drum tilted or flat. To achieve clear articulation, you may want to place a cloth or small towel over a portion of the head. The dampening material can be clamped to the hoop to hold it in place. Experiment with the amount of material and how much of the head you're covering to find the desired degree of resonance. To articulate the rhythm without a cloth, students can experiment playing with harder mallets, dampening with the knee, and/or striking the drum closer to the center of the head.

Box 6.2a

CONCERT BASS DRUM AND RELATED EQUIPMENT

- A bass drum of approximately 28 by 13 inches (This is fine for a smaller band in an average-sized room.)
- A tilting bass drum stand (Ideally, your bass drum stand will be able to position the drum both vertically and horizontally. While rhythms and rolls *can* be played on a drum in either position, your students may find it easier—and they may play with more precision—when the drum is set flat.)

RECOMMENDED MALLETS
- One large, general purpose bass drum mallet
- A pair of lighter, smaller bass drum mallets for rolling and playing rhythmic passages

Suspended and Crash Cymbals

SUSPENDED CYMBALS
Match Mallets to Cymbals

Tympani mallets should not be used to strike cymbals. With an outer felt that is too soft and a core that is too hard, you hear too much of a hit on the attack. Unless the score calls specifically for another type of mallet (sometimes composers call for a snare drum stick on the cymbal), your school should ideally have several pairs of yarn mallets, of different weights and thicknesses, to work properly with various sizes of cymbals. Have your students experiment with the sounds they're getting from different cymbal and mallet combinations. Don't let them use the cymbal that happens to be nearest at hand. Choosing the right cymbal and mallets should be based on musical considerations.

Playing Single Notes on the Cymbal

Students often strike the cymbal too close to the bell, producing too much attack and not enough sustained ring. The cymbal should be struck at its edge to achieve its optimal effect.

Note that larger cymbals do not respond as quickly to a stroke as smaller cymbals. Before striking a larger cymbal, it is commonly "warmed up" by tapping it lightly and *quietly* with the fingers or a soft mallet.

As always, in order to achieve maximum vibration and an open sound, the mallet is dropped rather than hammered into the cymbal, and lifted off in a single, fluid motion.

Dampening the Cymbal

Suspended cymbals are dampened by grabbing the edge of the cymbal with one or two hands. Percussionists may want to *partially* dampen a cymbal when, for example, cymbal notes are played close together and greater articulation is desired.

If a tie attached to a cymbal note is not attached to a subsequent note, the cymbal should be allowed to continue ringing. (You may find "l.v."— *laissez vibrer*—or simply "let ring" written in the part as well).

While students should pay close attention to note lengths and rests – especially when playing pieces for the first time—keep in mind that cymbal parts are often not carefully written. Experienced percussionists are given some leeway when it comes to interpreting them. As your students mature musically and listen to the sounds they are creating more carefully, they should feel freer to use the notation as a guideline, and allow their ears and musicality a greater role in informing their interpretation of the parts.

Suspended Cymbal Roll

Playing a roll on a cymbal might appear easy, but rarely have I met a high school percussionist who got it right. Attention to the following points will afford your students greater control and have them producing more musical sounds from the suspended cymbal.

To achieve an optimal suspended cymbal roll, the mallets are placed opposite each other on the left and right sides of the cymbal, striking at the edge.

The bigger the cymbal is, the slower the roll. Rolling too quickly on a cymbal kills the sound. Have your students experiment with how slowly they can play a roll to sustain the sound.

As with all percussion playing, if the mallets or sticks are not dropped from the same height above the instrument, one of the strokes will be accented, resulting in an uneven cymbal roll.

Practicing Rolls

Exercise 6.3a Ending a roll on a note

(a)

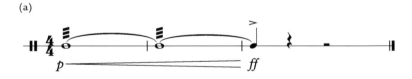

Have your students practice rolling slowly over one or two bars, starting *piano* and ending *double forte*. The roll shouldn't be played too quickly and the crescendo should be even. In Exercise 6.3a, the quarter note at the beginning of the third bar should be struck exactly on the downbeat and given its full note value before being dampened.

Exercise 6.3b Ending a roll with no downbeat

If a cymbal roll ends without a downbeat, as in Exercise 6.3b, it must be sustained right up to the beginning of the following rest and dampened cleanly.

Box 6.3a

SUSPENDED CYMBALS AND RELATED EQUIPMENT

- Medium (to thin) cymbals

Thick cymbals are less sensitive than thinner cymbals. They may be appropriate for rock drumming, but not for use as an orchestral suspended cymbal. Medium and thin cymbals are more versatile choices for all-around use. The thinner the cymbal, the quicker it "speaks" when struck, but be aware that thin cymbals are not as robust; if played too hard, they may not stand up over time.

- 16-inch to 22-inch sizes

When buying a new suspended cymbal, look for one with a quicker response and a longer decay. If your budget allows for one cymbal only, an 18-inch, medium-weight cymbal is a versatile choice.

The drum set ride cymbal may be as small as 18 inches. You'll more commonly find 20-inch ride cymbals and 16-inch crash cymbals (22-inch rides and 18-inch crashes can sound fine but may be unnecessarily large).

RECOMMENDED MALLETS
- Medium soft yarn mallets for general playing
- Medium hard mallets for greater articulation

A pair of soft and hard yarn mallets would also be desirable to achieve certain effects.

SUSPENDED CYMBAL STANDS AND SO FORTH
- Suspended cymbal stands for drum set and concert work

Regular, pole-type stands are most often used in schools where they serve double duty for concert work and at the drum set. They tend to rattle if not kept in top shape. Gooseneck stands are excellent for band and orchestra. They allow the cymbal to resonate more than regular stands and tend to rattle less, but they can't double on a drum set and, depending on the model, you'll have to attach a strap to the cymbal to suspend it.

- Extra cymbal felt*
- Extra rubber cymbal sleeves (to prevent the cymbal from scraping against the metal)*
- Extra metal cup washers to support the cymbal if the sleeve and cup are not a single piece*

On regular stands, cymbals are supported with metal or plastic plates (cup washers) topped with a thick layer of felt. Rubber or plastic cymbal sleeves run through the felt and the cymbal, and a wing nut is screwed on at the top of the stand. Be sure to keep replacement cup washers, felt, and cymbal sleeves on hand, and check stands regularly for worn or missing parts. These are very important. Without them, the cymbal not only will produce a less than optimal sound but also may eventually end up with cracks and/or a badly damaged center hole.

For regular stands.

CRASH CYMBALS
Holding the Cymbals

To hold a crash cymbal, the strap is grasped with the thumb and index finger close to the bell of the cymbal (Illustration 6.3a). With the thumb on top, the index finger bears the cymbal's weight. The hand takes the form of a fist as the remaining fingers curl around the *outside* of the hanging strap. *Students should not place their fingers inside the strap.* Doing so inhibits the sound production and makes it more difficult and time consuming to pick the cymbals up or put them down when switching to and from other instruments.

Illustration 6.3a Holding the crash cymbals.

(a)

Crash Cymbal Technique

Playing a Single Crash

To play a single crash, the cymbals are held at a slight angle, usually with the top of the cymbals to the left. The hands are set at a height corresponding more or less to the base of the rib cage. The shoulders are relaxed and the elbows are close to the body.

The cymbal in the right hand is held at a more acute angle, bringing the top edges of the cymbals closer together than the bottom edges. To prepare the crash, the arms pull the cymbals away from each other, maintaining the angles of the cymbals. When the cymbals are thrown together, the top of the right-hand cymbal strikes the top of the lower cymbal about an inch from its outer edge a fraction of a second before the bulk of the two cymbals clash together. This creates an effect much like a flam. Having the cymbals offset in this way ensures that no air pockets—which at best kill the sound and at worst lock the cymbals together—are created. In the follow-through movement, the cymbals are lifted slightly upward as they are pulled apart.

To muffle the cymbals, they are drawn into the chest. Unless indicated, students must listen carefully to the rest of the orchestra and make a musical decision as to how long the cymbals should ring before muffling them.

Playing Quick Repeated Crashes

To play quick repeated crashes called for in marches (as well as concert music), it's important to play with a pair of lighter cymbals.

The cymbals are held as described earlier, but at a less acute angle and closer to each other before releasing them for each attack. As the crashes may repeat for extended periods of time—in the case of marches especially—remind your students to stand with a straight back, relaxing the muscles in the shoulder and neck, and moving the cymbals together with quick movements from the elbows.

Box 6.3b

CRASH CYMBALS AND RELATED EQUIPMENT

- Two medium 16-inch cymbals for general playing (Thin cymbals would be easier to control for younger students, but keep in mind they are not as durable.)
- A larger pair (18 to 20 inches) for louder crashes

REQUIRED ACCESSORIES
- Proper cymbal straps (and straps only. Pads designed to protect the knuckles are unnecessary and just deaden the sound. Never use wood handles.)

Note: See companion website ⏵ for directions on tying crash cymbal straps.

- Crash cymbal stand

CHAPTER 6.4

The Tambourine

TAMBOURINE PERFORMANCE: THE NUMBER ONE MISTAKE

The most common mistake high school percussion students make when playing the tambourine is that they swing it toward the free hand to play a note. This results in superfluous jingle sound before the impact. If a series of notes are being played, the repeated swinging back and forth can produce so much jingling that the rhythm itself cannot be heard.

The tambourine should remain stationary and at about a 45-degree angle when struck with the free hand.

THE BASIC STROKES
Playing with One Hand

To play quiet to moderately loud passages with one hand, the tambourine is held at roughly a 45-degree angle in the nondominant hand at about chest height. The head is struck with the fingertips of the free hand, which are pulled together (Illustration 6.4a). For lighter sections, the instrument is struck toward the edge of the head.

For the most delicate sections, where you want a dry, crisp jingle sound with no ring off the head, the student should rest the heel of the striking hand lightly near the center of the head and tap the edge of the instrument with either the tip of the middle finger or the tips of the middle and index fingers.

For loud passages, the hand is made into a fist, and the center of the instrument is struck solidly with the flat part of the curved fingers and the heel of the hand.

Illustration 6.4a Striking the tambourine with the fingertips.

(a)

Playing Rapid Passages with Two Hands

There are two ways to support the tambourine when playing rhythmic passages that are too quick to be played with one hand.

It can be placed on a soft base, such as a piece of foam or a folded towel set on a percussion table. With the forearms, just above the wrists, placed on top of the tambourine to control its movement, the front part of the instrument is struck with the outstretched fingers.

An alternative method is to rest a foot on the rung of a chair and place the tambourine upside down on the extended thigh, which is now parallel to the floor (Illustration 6.4b). The instrument is again secured by the forearms, just above the wrist, resting on the frame. Rhythms are played with the four fingers of each hand, outstretched and extended over the far edge of the tambourine frame.

Illustration 6.4b The tambourine is placed on the thigh to play quick rhythms.

Playing Loud, Fast Passages

For loud, fast rhythmic passages, the tambourine can be played using the hand and knee.

With the dominant-side foot resting on a stool so that the thigh is parallel to the floor, the tambourine is held face down with the dominant hand. By sandwiching the tambourine between the knee and the other hand— made into a fist—rhythms are performed by moving the tambourine up and down, striking the instrument alternately with the knee and the fist. It's a technique often used to play the *Trepak* in Tchaikovsky's Nutcracker ballet, to mention one well-known example.

ROLLS

Tambourine rolls may be played two ways: with a shake roll, which is louder, or with a finger roll.

The Shake Roll

To produce a shake roll, the tambourine is held in the nondominant hand at about a 45-degree angle, with the forearm extended parallel to the floor. The jingles are set into play by rapidly rotating the wrist.

To cleanly articulate the beginning and end of the roll, the instrument is struck with the free hand. Care must be taken not to play accents unless they are written.

For a quieter roll, the forearm is dropped, and the tambourine is shaken from a lower position at the side of the body. A crescendo roll is begun with the tambourine held in the quieter position and gradually lifted to a position as high as eye level. For a decrescendo, the instrument is moved from the higher to the lower level.

Note that rolls must end with the tambourine in a horizontal position so that the jingles are flat and don't sound when the instrument is set aside.

The Finger Roll

To execute very quiet rolls, finger rolls are required. These are played by sliding either the top of the thumb or the tip of the middle finger along the top edge of the head (Illustration 6.4c).

Illustration 6.4c Playing a finger roll with the thumb.

Box 6.4a

RECOMMENDED TAMBOURINES

- A good-quality 10-inch tambourine with a head, a double row of jingles, and a wood shell is a good choice for general concert playing. One with a single row of jingles is generally better for more delicate passages, as well as for younger students with smaller hands. Eight-inch tambourines are also available.
- A round or crescent-shaped, headless tambourine for pop or Latin music

If you only have one tambourine, make sure it is round, is relatively light, and has a head. Tambourines with no head—be they round or crescent shaped—are fine for playing eighth notes in a rhythm section, but they produce little impact in the concert band when you need to hear single tambourine notes played at a forte level.

The tambourine head should be prepared by applying a thin layer of beeswax or violin rosin along its outside edge to make it slightly tacky. Students can also try moistening the finger with a quick lick of the tongue just before playing the roll to produce greater resistance between the finger and head. Gliding the finger lightly along the edge of the head, without too much pressure, should result in an even, dense roll.

The Triangle and Sleigh Bells

THE TRIANGLE
Suspending/Holding the Triangle

A triangle is usually suspended from a single clip that is held at eye level in the nondominant hand.

For a right-handed player, it is positioned with the open end on the left side (Illustration 6.5a).

The clip is supported by the thumb and middle finger, with the fourth and fifth fingers poised to curl down and dampen the triangle when necessary.

To play quick rhythmic patterns using two beaters, the triangle should be suspended from two clips, one at each of the closed corners, which are clamped to the music stand.

Striking the Triangle

The desired triangle sound is complex, with lots of overtones rather than a clear pitch.

When playing a triangle suspended from a single clip, striking it along the side will cause it to swing back and forth more than striking it along the bottom. Your percussionists should experiment hitting it in different spots—in the middle of an arm or closer to the corners—to find the best sound. After striking the instrument, the beater should immediately be pulled back to allow it to vibrate freely.

Illustration 6.5a Holding the triangle.

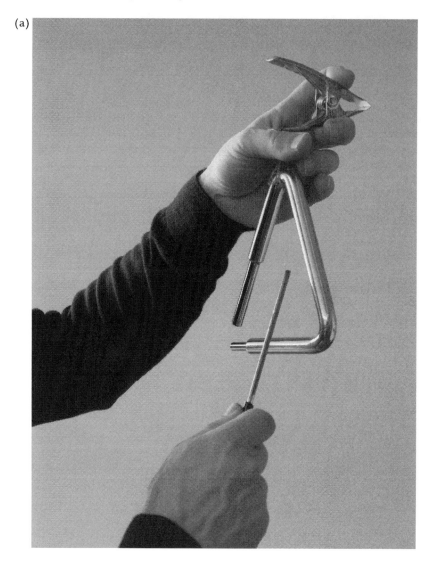

(a)

Rolls are played by placing the beater in either the top or bottom closed corner of the instrument and rapidly striking the triangle between the two sides.

When the triangle is suspended from two clips, it is struck along the top side.

To play quieter passages or rolls, lighter, thinner beaters should be used.

Box 6.5a
TRIANGLES AND RELATED EQUIPMENT

- Good-quality triangles, ranging from 6 to 10 inches (Don't buy cheap triangles—they sound dead compared to instruments suitable for concert performance.)
- A quality set of metal beaters, ranging from thick to thin (Triangles should not be struck with a snare stick. It produces a "bang" when it strikes the instrument and doesn't bring out the desired complex overtones.)
- Triangle clips; thin strong line to suspend the triangle from the clip (Fishing line works well. Thick line dulls the sound. *Make sure that an independent safety line is added.* It will be longer and hang loose around the top of the triangle to catch the instrument in case the main line breaks.)

SLEIGH BELLS

Sleigh bells are generally held upside down and gripped firmly in the fist of the nondominant hand. The thumb and index finger are in line with or *slightly* above the end of the handle, which is struck with either the palm of the opened, dominant hand or the side of the hand drawn into a fist.

Sleigh bells are very sensitive to any motion, and care must be taken when picking them up and setting them down. This *can* be done quietly—though moving the bells should be avoided during quieter moments of a piece. An alternate method of playing them, which will help keep unnecessary jingling to a minimum, is to pick them up while keeping them parallel to the floor and to strike the bells directly on the side of the instrument.

PART 7

Latin Percussion

Introduction: Latin Percussion

Latin or Latin-flavored music is a staple in orchestral, concert, and stage band repertoire, and it is indeed rare to find a school that does not have at least one hand drum and a smattering of smaller Latin percussion accessories in its music room. It is less common, however, to find students or teachers paying any serious attention to the techniques of playing conga or any other type of hand drum.

It's not that every concert percussionist needs to play hand drums at a professional level; even most orchestral percussionists don't. But to achieve at least an approximation of the distinctive tones and rhythms that are found at the heart of Latin music, a few basic techniques must be considered.

Keep in mind too that, as with all auxiliary percussion, the smaller Latin instruments such as the guiro, cabasa, and maracas must not be taken for granted. Indeed, they are essential components of the Latin sound, and no performance of this music will be successful if they are not played with energy, conviction, and exacting rhythmic precision.

The Conga Drum

THE BACKGROUND
Tumbao and the Four Main Tones

Conga drummers typically coax myriad tones from their instruments through a variety of techniques. We will limit ourselves here to the open, slap, bass, and finger tones, the four tones required to perform the basic Latin dance rhythm pattern called *tumbao*. Students should listen to recordings of the different tones and model the sounds they produce accordingly.

Terminology

To avoid confusion, here is a word about terminology.

In English, what we refer to as a collection of different-sized "conga drums" is, in the Spanish-speaking world, called "tumbadora," and in Spanish, the three most common drums are called, from largest to smallest, the tumba, the conga, and the quinto. Throughout this section, the singular "conga" specifically refers to the middle-sized drum.

Tuning

When a pair of drums are being played, they are commonly tuned in fourths. The pitches need not be exact, but in general, tune the conga roughly to a "C" and the lower tumba to a "G." If the conga is paired with the higher quinto, tune the quinto to an "F." (When a set of three drums are played, they are typically tuned to "G," "C," and "E.")

Box 7.2a
CONGA DRUMS AND RELATED EQUIPMENT

• One or two conga drums

One drum is all that is necessary to play basic Latin rhythms, but in modern orchestras, two drums are more common.

Wood drums have a warmer sound and are often the choice of pros, but fiberglass drums are a good choice; they produce a brighter and louder sound, are a little easier to play, do not react to environmental changes, and tend to be lighter than wood. Synthetic heads are recommended; skin heads are too sensitive to changes in humidity. Full-sized congas are approximately 12.5 inches (tumba), 11.75 inches (conga), and 11 inches (quinto).

If you're buying one instrument, you'll want the conga. The second drum is typically the tumba, though some may prefer the higher-pitched quinto. Entry-level drums are smaller, usually sold in 10-inch and 11-inch sizes, and are also a good choice, especially for younger students.

• Stands for each drum or a double stand

Traditional conga drummers play seated, but in a concert setting, you should have stands.

TEACHING THE FUNDAMENTALS
Positioning the Body

The congas should be placed so that the player, with shoulders relaxed, can extend the forearms comfortably from the elbows to form a 90-degree angle. In playing position, one should be able to draw a straight line from the tips of the fingers to the elbow.

When playing with two congas, the larger drum is typically placed to the right of the smaller drum.

The Open Tone

Exercise 7.2a The open tone.

(a)

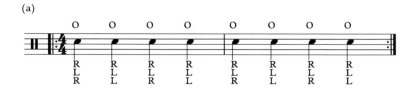

The open tone is the tone that sings. With the wrists flat and the four fingers held together, the hand is positioned with the base of the fingers lined up along the edge of the drum head. The hand, staying relaxed, is lifted off the drum from the wrist and dropped onto the head. Immediately after the four fingers strike the head, the wrist pulls them back up off the drum, allowing it to ring (Illustration 7.2a).

Illustration 7.2a The bases of the fingers line up along the conga's bearing edge; the arms are at a 90-degree angle.

(a)

The Slap Tone

Exercise 7.2b The slap tone.

(b)

The slap tone is a sharp crack that cuts unmistakably through the rest of the ensemble. The hand is positioned more deeply into the drum than it is for an open tone, with the middle of the palm roughly in line with the edge of the head. The important difference between the slap and the open tone is that with the slap, the only parts of the hand that strike the head are the pads at the ends of the fingers.

To do this, the fingers must be relaxed and allowed to form a gentle curve. When the relaxed hand is lifted and dropped, the tips of the fingers strike the drum, remaining "stuck" on the head. Think of a soaking wet towel being dropped onto the floor. You also might think of the ends of the fingers gripping the head at the moment of impact.

Keep in mind that you're listening for a different *quality* of sound from the slap and not necessarily more volume.

The Bass Tone

Exercise 7.2c The bass tone.

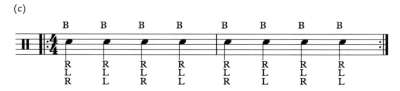

The bass tone may be used to play the heel tone of a tumbao rhythm played at a slower tempo. To execute this low, dull tone, the drum is struck toward the center of the head. With the hand opened and the fingers held together and turned up, the palm is dropped flat onto the drum. While some fingers may lightly contact the head, the fundamental bass tone is created through the contact with the palm.

The Heel Tone

The heel tone is used for a tumbao played at any tempo. It is similar to a bass tone, but with an open hand, the drum is struck only by the fleshy part across the bottom of the palm.

The Finger or Touch Tone

The finger or touch tone is produced when the fingertips, held together, are dropped onto the drum. The fingers rest on the head, muffling the sound. The touch tone differs from the slap as it is a light tone. Played with the left hand along with the heel tone, it is an important component of the tumbao.

Tumbao

Exercise 7.2d Tumbao (single drum).

(d)

Exercise 7.2e Tumbao (two drums).

(e)

Tumbao is one of the most commonly played rhythms on conga drums, suitable for a variety of Latin dance styles. Originally, conga players used only a single drum, as in Exercise 7.2d, and you can definitely use one drum to perform any conga parts that are required. Should you have two drums, your students can practice the two-bar pattern, shown in Exercise 7.2e. This particular figure corresponds to the 3:2 son clave pattern (see chapter 3.4, *Latin Drumming*, Example 3.4a, page 101).

Other Latin Percussion

L ike the auxiliary percussion instruments discussed earlier, some of the smaller Latin percussion instruments commonly found in music rooms—such as the bongos, guiros, castanets, maracas, and claves discussed here—don't get the respect they deserve. To hear these instruments played well, however, is truly eye-opening.

By paying attention to the fundamental techniques presented here, your students should begin to play these instruments with a better tone quality, more character, and greater effect.

THE BONGO DRUMS

Bongo drums are traditionally played seated and held between the legs. In a concert situation, it's more common to see them placed on a stand, with the larger drum (the female or "hembra" drum in Spanish) to the right of the smaller drum (the male or "macho" drum).

While their performance has much in common with that of conga drums, the fingers play a more important role due to the bongos' size and high pitch.

The Tones

The Open Tone

The main tone played on the bongos is the "open" tone, which can be executed by the index finger alone or by the index finger along with the third and fourth fingers, depending on the sound quality desired. The drum is struck toward the edge, with the fingers bouncing up immediately after striking it, allowing for as much ring as possible. Different sounds are achieved by using the top third of the finger through to the full finger.

The Muffled Tone

The muffled tone is basically an open tone where the fingers remain on the head at the end of the stroke.

The Thumb Tone

To execute the thumb tone, the thumb, extended from base to tip, strikes across the center of the head through a turn of the wrist. It remains on the head, creating a muffled sound.

The Fingertip Tone

The fingertip tone is produced with a turn of the wrist toward the fingertips. This too is a muffled tone.

The Martillo

The "martillo," which means "hammer" in Spanish, is a primary rhythmic pattern played on the bongos.

Exercise 7.3a The martillo

(a)

M = Muffled F = Fingertips T = Thumb O = Open

Beginning with the left thumb resting on the smaller drum, the first muffled stroke is played with the first joint of the right-hand index finger at the edge of the drum. This is followed with a left-hand finger stroke, another right-hand muffled stroke, then a thumb stroke. The pattern is basically repeated for the second half of the bar, except that the stroke on beat four is an open stroke played on the large drum.

Note that by playing a muffled stroke on beat two with the finger placed more deeply toward the center of the drum, the pattern is given a more interesting shape.

THE GUIRO

The traditional guiro is a gourd, with holes cut on one side where it is held with the fingers. The opposite side has ridges cut along the length of the instrument. It is played by drawing a wood or metal scraper up or down across its length.

Wooden and synthetic instruments are readily available, with the synthetic instruments being the better choice when it comes to durability.

Exercise 7.3b Guiro patterns.

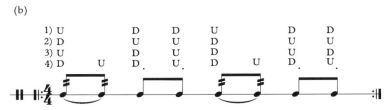

(b)

D = downstroke (away from the body) U = upstroke (toward the body)

There are several ways to play the basic guiro pattern in Exercise 7.3b.

The first pattern has a long upstroke played on the first and third beats and two short downstrokes on the eighth notes. Each downstroke is executed with a short, quick snap of the wrist. The sticking for the second pattern simply reverses the direction of the strokes in pattern one. Some may prefer playing the third pattern, which alternates between the up- and downstroke.

For the fourth sticking pattern, the first and third quarter-note beats are played as a single, flowing down- and upstroke. This pattern slightly changes the quality of the quarter note and is more of a challenge to play smoothly.

THE CASTANETS

While castanets are traditionally held in the hand and played with the fingers—a style associated with the colorful flamenco dancers of

Spain—when played by percussionists in bands and orchestras, they are usually mounted on handles or on castanet machines.

When mounted on handles, the percussionist holds them as he or she does snare drumsticks. Patterns are played by striking the castanets on the thigh, which is lifted to a position parallel to the floor by placing a foot on a low stool or another appropriate accessory.

When playing castanet machines, the castanet is struck lightly using only one or two fingers. Machines, which are played on a table, are particularly helpful in a multiple percussion context if there is little time to pick up and quietly put down a pair of castanets on handles.

Tremolos (rolls) on paddles are played with rapidly alternating wrist movements. On machines, they can be played as single-stroke rolls. Ambitious students may opt for a more authentic sound by striking the edge of each castanet with the fingertips, using a wavelike motion from the pinky to the index finger, and alternating hands.

To add further authenticity to castanet parts, quarter notes are commonly interpreted as flams.

THE MARACAS

Whether they're playing a precise rhythm or a steady groove, students will find it a challenge to play maracas cleanly and accurately. Not only is there a delay between the wrist/arm motion and the attack of any given note, but also the beads rolling around inside maracas are difficult to control and can easily muddy everything up.

Maracas are held much like drumsticks, with the thumb and index finger placed at the base of the bell. They are played with a sharp up/down movement of the wrist accompanied by some movement of the forearm. But if downbeats are generally played with the downstroke, keep in mind that when the maraca is swung up in preparation of the downbeat, the beads are easily thrown against the top of the instrument, delivering two notes for the price of one. This gives us a choice: to incorporate the stroke on the upswing into the rhythm or to play single notes only on the downstroke.

Exercise 7.3c Single notes.

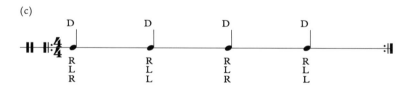

To play clear, single notes on maracas, either one or both maracas are held parallel to the floor with a firm grip. The hand motion combines a very short, downward snap of the wrist with a quick grab at the handle by the fingers, carefully timed so that the beads land precisely when they should.

The beads should be thrown against the inside wall of the head such that a clear attack is heard.

Alternatively, when playing at a quiet to medium volume, single notes can be produced by striking the maraca with the index finger. To do so, the maraca is held firmly and parallel to the floor, and the index finger is simply lifted and dropped onto the upper part of the handle, near where it meets the head.

Note: Exercises 7.3c to 7.3e should be practiced hands separately and hands together.

Exercise 7.3d Double notes: shuffle.

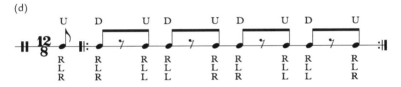

The position in which the maracas are held determines whether double notes—incorporating the sound of the beads striking the top of the maraca—will sound as a broken triplet pattern or even eighth notes.

To play a broken triplet pattern at slow to moderate tempos, the maracas are held in a horizontal position (parallel to the floor) and are lifted and dropped from the wrist.

Exercise 7.3e Double notes: even.

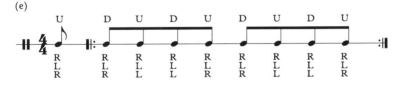

To play even eighth notes, the maracas are held perpendicular to the floor and swung back and forth so that, as much as possible, the beads fly from front to back inside the head rather than slide back and forth into each note. The goal is to hear the eighths attacked as cleanly as possible.

Exercise 7.3f Combination single/double-note pattern.

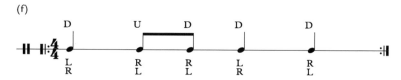

This exercise combines single- and double-note patterns. When played at a quicker tempo and with the hands at the horizontal position, you will hear even eighths.

CLAVES

Though you will find many claves today manufactured from synthetic materials, traditionally they are two cylindrical pieces of wood. The cylinders may be identical, or they may consist of a single cylinder paired with a larger one that is hollowed out with a section carved out of its underside. The hollowed-out clave produces a louder sound.

Depending on the style of instrument you have, either the plain or hollowed-out cylinder (with the carved section facing the palm) is held between the thumb and the fingers of the nondominant hand. The clave runs diagonally across the hand from the base of the index finger and rests on the heel of the hand. The palm, to create a sound chamber, should be cupped, and the grip should be loose.

The second clave, held toward its base like a snare drumstick, strikes the center of the first clave.

PART 8

Instrument Storage and Maintenance

Storing the Instruments

There are a number of reasons your percussion equipment should be stored neatly and in compartments that are clearly labeled.

The first, obviously, is so that students coming into class can easily find the instruments needed. Valuable time is often lost when percussionists raise their hand to ask you where the tambourine or wood block might be—just as you're ready to give the downbeat. And while having clearly labeled shelves and drawers does not guarantee that the instruments will be returned to them at the end of class, the goal is that, over time, your students get into the habit of returning things to where they belong.

The second reason is that your making an effort to maintain a neatly organized section sends a message to your students that the instruments have value and are to be respected. So, have a proper drawer assigned, for example, to the tambourine—and *never* allow it to be left on top of the timpani.

Finally, by keeping things organized, you will much more easily be able to assess the state of your percussion inventory. Though no system is perfect—and no matter what you do, small instruments may still show up months after you've bought replacements—maintaining a well-organized, well-labeled storage system is vastly superior to having a couple of drawers and some shelves set aside for students to dump haphazardly whatever instruments they happen to have been playing.

STORING STICKS AND MALLETS

Whether or not your students are responsible for bringing their own sticks and mallets to class, you will need extra pairs on hand.

You can keep them in a drawer, or store them standing on end in a large, cylindrical container – a method you might find allows for easier access.

Be sure that you have matched pairs of drumsticks, and that your students actually *play* with matched pairs during class. Two sticks – even if they are the same model from the same manufacturer – don't necessarily sound the same, and sometimes they can draw very different tone qualities from the drum. Higher quality drumsticks are carefully matched and sold in pairs.

Since you will likely store a few pairs of drumsticks together, consider color-coding matching pairs of the same model with markers in a spot away from where they are gripped so that students can easily pick them out.

Keyboard mallets do not pose the same concerns. There is virtually no difference among mallets of the same model.

Finally, you might want to keep a couple of extra triangle beaters in your desk along with an extra pair of timpani mallets. Small, metal beaters can get lost, and the felt heads of timpani mallets can become worn relatively quickly if they are not taken care of. Having extra beaters and mallets in your office will not only come in handy in case of an emergency; the need to draw upon them will also serve as a timely signal to call the music store for some necessary replacements.

Replacing and Tuning Drum Heads

THE BACKGROUND

For drums to sound good, you *must* pay attention to their tuning—a fact that is too often ignored in the classroom.

Drum heads should not be cranked up to the point that they sound choked, nor should they be loosened to the point that they produce a dull "thud." And for any drum—be it a tom-tom, snare drum, bass drum, or timpani—to truly "sing," the drum must be in tune with itself, with each of the tension rods exerting an equal amount of pressure on the head to produce the same, sustained, clear, and unwavering pitch. The process of bringing the head in tune with itself is called fine-tuning or "clearing" the head.

Drum heads stretch and go out of tune under normal wear and tear, so they should be fine-tuned from time to time, but once a drum or timpani head has dents—timp heads in particular—good tuning becomes impossible and the head must be replaced.

THE FUNDAMENTALS
Replacing and Tuning Drum Heads

When listening for the quality of a drum tuning, you want to hear a clear tone, with a sound that is open and sustained. Tuning tom-toms to a specific pitch is not necessary, though some percussionists—especially those playing drum set—like to do so.

If you don't need to replace a head and simply want to fine-tune, skip to the section *Fine-Tuning Tom-Toms*.

Replacing and Tuning Tom-Tom Heads

The information presented in *Replacing and Tuning Tom-Tom Heads,* applies in general to snare drum and timpani, but because head replacement for those drums has specific challenges, you will find additional information on those instruments elsewhere in this chapter.

1. Unscrew all the tension rods, remove the metal hoop with the head attached, and pop out the plastic head.
2. Wipe clean the bearing edge of the shell, the inside of the drum, and the lugs on the outside of the drum.
3. Check that all screws inside of the drum are tight.
4. Check for dirt on the tension rods. You may want to wipe each rod with a soft cloth, then dab a little Vaseline on the ends when it comes time to screw them back in.
5. Place the new head on the drum, and put the metal hoop on top, with the holes in the hoop lined up with those of the lugs. *Note: When replacing the bottom hoop of a snare drum, make sure that the openings are lined up with the throw-off and snare butt.*
6. Insert the tension rods through the hoops and screw them into the lugs by hand until they are finger tight.
7. Continue tightening the tension rods by half-turns using the drum key, in the order shown in Illustration 8.2a. (If there are more or fewer tension rods, tighten them following a similar pattern.) After each complete tightening cycle around the head, press down with the palm of your hand on the center of the drum head to set it. Check the pitch as you raise the tension on the head, and use smaller turns of the drum key as you approach the target pitch. Once you have reached a pitch you are happy with, you may have to fine-tune, or clear, the drum head (see *Fine-Tuning [Clearing] Tom-Toms* later).
8. Tuning both tom tom heads to the same pitch provides the purest tone and the most resonance, but whether they are tuned to the same pitch, or the bottom head is tuned higher or lower relative to the top head is a question of personal taste. I recommend that you first tune both heads to the same pitch—one with good sustain—making sure they are not too loose nor so tight that they sound choked, and experiment from there. If you like the feel of the batter head, try loosening or tightening the resonant head to change the timbre and pitch if desired. For the relative tuning of snare drum heads, see *Replacing and Tuning Snare Drum Heads* later.

Fine-Tuning (Clearing) Tom-Toms
To fine-tune a tom-tom:

1. Lightly tap the head with a finger about 1 inch from the edge of the drum in front of each lug. Listen carefully as you check and make note

Illustration 8.2a Tension rod tuning order.

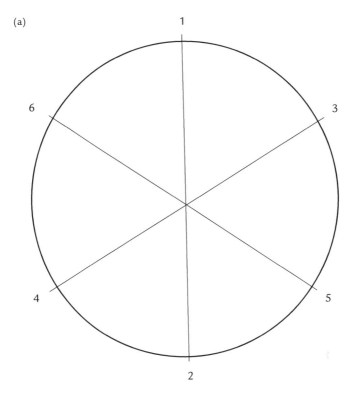

of the pitches at the different tension points around the drum. Many find the use of a Drumdial—an instrument that measures the tension on the head—helpful with this process.

2. Loosen or tighten the out-of-tune lugs to even out the tension. Again, you must regularly press down on the center of the drum with your palm while tuning to set the head.

3. Check the pitch of the drum once the head is cleared. If it's higher or lower than desired, adjust the tension rods accordingly using small and equal turns of the key.

Replacing and Tuning Snare Drum Heads

To replace and tune snare drum heads, follow the steps outlined in *Replacing Tom-Tom Heads*, keeping in mind that when replacing the counterhoop on the bottom head, the openings in the hoop are lined up with the throw-off and snare butt.

Also, note that the two heads of the snare drum (illustrations 8.2b and 8.2c) work together differently than those on tom-toms.

Illustration 8.2b Snare drum: top view.

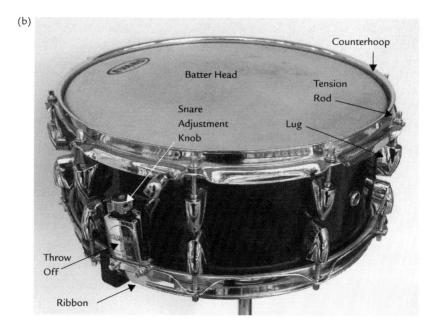

Illustration 8.2c Snare drum: bottom view.

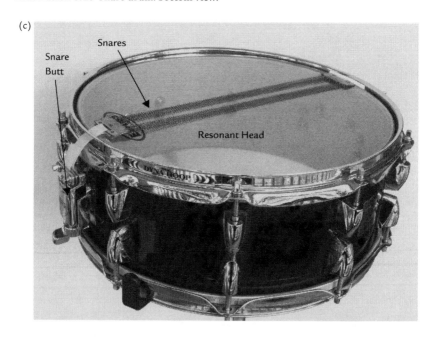

The purpose of the thin, bottom (resonant) head is to interact with the snares to produce a sensitive share response. To do so, it must be tuned tight. The resonant heads—as well as the batter heads—on school snare drums are often tuned much too low, leaving them with a tubby sound and without the crispness and snap required of a well-tuned instrument.

You'll find that even experts differ enormously regarding the relative tuning of the top and bottom snare drum heads. In general, if you tune both heads to about a "G" and then slightly raise the pitch of the resonant head, your snare should sound fine.

Removing and Replacing the Snares

To change the bottom head, the snares too must be removed and replaced. To remove the snares:

1. Turn the snare drum upside down. Depending on the throw-off design, either string or ribbon is used to attach the snares to the throw-off and the "snare butt"—the clamp on the side of the drum opposite the throw-off. Whatever the system, loosen the screws, carefully remove the snares, and put them aside until after the head is replaced.
2. Replace and tune the head as explained in *Replacing and Tuning Tom-Tom Heads*, points 1 to 7, earlier.

To replace the snares:

1. Make sure the snare throw-off is in the off (lowered) position and set the adjustment knob roughly midway between the tightest and loosest tension position.
2. Set the snares in place on the drum head and thread the strings or plastic strip through the hoop and the holes or clasps in the throw-off and snare butt. Note: The snares must ultimately be centered when they are lifted to make contact with the head. Lifting the snares may pull them toward the strainer, so at this point place the snares slightly closer to the butt. (It may still be necessary to make adjustments later.)
3. Tighten the screws on the butt, then the strainer, making the tension on the string or ribbon fairly tight.
4. Turn the drum over. With the snare throw-off still lowered (in the off position), the snares should not be engaged with the head. Lift the throw-off, and tighten the snares with the adjustment knob so that they engage with the head. *Do not overtighten the snares; doing so chokes the sound of the drum.*
5. If you are unable to tighten the snares sufficiently using the adjustment knob, you will have to remove the snares and return to point 2,

readjusting the strings or strips so that the snares can be pulled tighter against the head. Conversely, if the snares at their loosest tension are so tight that they block the strainer from lifting fully into place, you will have to return to point 2 and make sure that the strings or strips are attached more loosely to the throw-off and snare butt.

Replacing and Tuning Timpani Heads

Replacing Timpani Heads

The following directions apply to timpani with balanced action pedals— the instruments most commonly found in schools—where the pedal pivots like a see-saw to raise and lower the pitch (illustration 8.2d).

Illustration 8.2d The timpani.

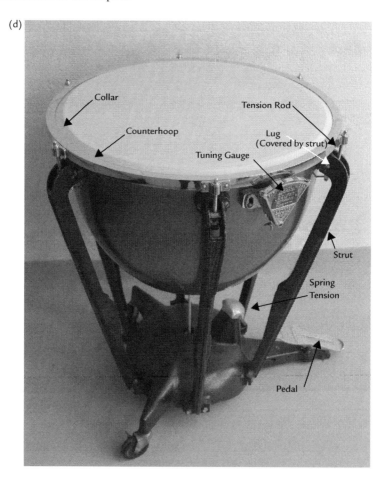

Note: When ordering new timpani heads, be aware that head sizes are determined differently from those of other drums. Many timpani heads have a collar that extends beyond the rim of the drum, leaving a gap between the side of the drum and the counterhoop. In this case, you must purchase a head that is 2 inches larger than the size of the timpani: for a 26-inch drum you will need a 28-inch head, a 32-inch drum requires a 34-inch head, and so forth. There are exceptions to this rule, depending on the make of the drum and the year it was made, so the safest way to determine the correct size is by measuring the head that is being replaced before placing your order.

For the most part, the outline given in *Replacing Tom-Tom Heads* (earlier) applies to replacing timpani heads, but there are some important additional points you must keep in mind.

The materials needed to replace a timpani head are a block of wood, fine steel wool, masking tape, a felt-tip marker, cleaning solution, Vaseline or automotive grease, silicon spray, a timpani mallet, a timpani key, and rags. A Drumdial may be helpful.

1. Place one piece of tape on the counterhoop and then another directly below it on the bowl. Line up and mark spots on both pieces of tape so that you can later return the counterhoop to the exact same position over the bowl.
2. Using the pedal, bring the pitch of the head to its lowest position and place a wood block, or something else suitable, under the raised end of the pedal to ensure that it doesn't snap down while unscrewing the tension rods.
3. Unscrew the tension rods, one turn at a time on each rod as you move around the drum, until they can be removed from the lugs. Do not remove the tension rods from the counterhoop.
4. Lift the counterhoop, tension rods, and head off the bowl, and then remove and discard the old head.
5. Wipe the bottom surface of the counterhoop. If dirt has built up on the tension rods, remove and clean them one at a time, and then dab a little Vaseline or cork grease on the tips before returning them to the position on the counterhoop from which they were taken.
6. Wipe the inside of the bowl. If the bearing edge is not smooth, stroke it lightly with fine steel wool and cleaner—with a series of motions from the inside of the rim toward you rather than in a single, circular motion around the top of the drum. Wipe the bearing edge, and then spray it lightly with silicone.

7. Place the new timpani head on the bearing edge. When placing the new head on the drum:
   a. Place the head so that the label is opposite the playing area.
   b. Make sure that the head is centered and that the overhang of the head is even throughout the bowl's circumference.
8. Place the counterhoop and tension rods over the head, lining up the marks placed earlier on the counterhoop and bowl.
9. Screw the tension rods into the lugs by hand until they are finger tight. If there are wrinkles on the collar of the head, tighten the nearest tension rods until they flatten out.
10. Tune the drum up to the lowest pitch of its correct range (see chapter 5.1, *Introduction: Timpani*, page 151 for timpani ranges), tightening all the tension rods by half, quarter, or even smaller turns as you get closer to the targeted pitch. Tune in a pattern similar to that in Illustration 8.2a. After each cycle around the drum, set the head by pressing on its center with an open palm, and check the pitch by tapping the drum lightly with your finger. Continue until you reach the desired pitch.
11. Remove the wood block, and pedal up to a midrange note to begin clearing the head (see *Fine-Tuning (Clearing) Timpani Heads* below). Many people clear the head by ear, tapping it lightly with the middle finger about 2 inches in front of each lug and adjusting accordingly, but you may find the use of a Drumdial helpful.
12. With the head cleared, now check that the pedal is firmly holding the required pitches. To do so, check both the bottom and top of the instrument's range. Return the pedal to its lowest position, check the pitch, and make any tuning adjustments. Usually everything is okay; however, when the pitch is correct with the pedal pressed to the floor but creeps up when the foot is released, the tension on the spring adjustment must be loosened by turning the knob counterclockwise. Do this very carefully, turning the knob no more than a quarter turn at a time, and *be sure to reinsert the wood block under the front end of the pedal before doing so.* Loosening the spring too much can result in the rod becoming completely disengaged and the pedal violently snapping down to the floor. If it should disengage, you must raise the pedal to the highest position and try, through trial and error, to re-engage the rod. If, after tuning, the bottom note is holding on its own but the pitch dips down after pedaling to the top of the range, the tension on the spring adjustment must be tightened by turning the knob clockwise.

Fine-Tuning (Clearing) Timpani Heads

While you may be able to put up with a tom-tom that doesn't "sing," timpani that are not in tune with themselves—that don't produce a clear, sustained pitch—are unacceptable.

When each tuning point on the head produces the same pitch, the note produced when the drum is struck will be stable. Equalizing the pitch at each lug is called fine-tuning or "clearing" the head.

If your timpani heads have tears or dents, replace them. If they're in good condition but the pitch is not clear or unstable after a note is struck, you will need to do the following:

1. Pedal to a midrange pitch on the drum.
2. Strike the drum loudly. If the pitch dips immediately, you have to tighten one or more tension rods. If it rises after the initial tone is heard, you will have to loosen one or more tension rods. Frequently, a combination of tightening and loosening is necessary.
3. You can either tune by ear—and tuning timpani by ear is a challenge for even more experienced percussionists—or tune with the help of a Drumdial.
   a. To tune by ear: Listen to the fundamental pitch as you quietly tap the head about 3 to 4 inches in from the edge and in front of each lug. Tapping quietly allows you to hear more of the fundamental tone without bringing out more overtones. You'll have to go around the drum several times, checking, comparing, and adjusting pitches. Note that tuning timpani quickly tires the ear. Don't spend more than ten minutes tuning without taking a break.
   b. To tune with a Drumdial: Set the Drumdial on the head in front of each lug to get readings around the timpani. Tighten or loosen each tension rod accordingly to even out the tension around the drum.

CHAPTER 8.3

An Overview of Percussion Inventory and Instrument Maintenance

At the beginning of each school year, and every few months thereafter, you'll want to make sure that your percussion equipment is accounted for and in good working order. Your students will only learn to care for their instruments if they see that *you* place importance on their maintenance.

The following is a list of the basic equipment and mallets that you should have in your collection, and what you should look for when inspecting their state of repair or buying new instruments.

To help with taking stock of your percussion inventory, and organizing what repairs and purchases may be needed, see Appendix A, *Percussion Inventory and Repair Checklist*.

INSPECTING YOUR AUXILIARY PERCUSSION

Your collection of auxiliary percussion might include tambourines, wood blocks, triangles, maracas, castanets, claves, guiros, shakers, sleigh bells, whistles, slapsticks, and ratchets. Make a list of what you've got, and make sure that when the instruments are not in use they're stored in designated and clearly marked drawers and/or storage spaces. You may want to store some of the smaller, less frequently used instruments in your office.

A few points with regard to specific instruments and accessories:

Cymbals and Stands

- Check all cymbals for cracks. Check for worn center holes on your suspended cymbals. A cymbal *may* still be usable if the cracks are small or the center hole has not been worn too much.
- To prevent the cymbal damage described above, make sure that your cymbal stands have:
  1. the round metal plates (cup washers) and thick felt pads that rest underneath and support the cymbal, and
  2. plastic or nylon cymbal sleeves to prevent the cymbal from abrading against the metal of the stand.
- Keep a supply of cup washers, felt pads, and cymbal sleeves on hand and check regularly to see that none are missing from your stands. Without them, cymbals can become irreparably damaged.
- Check for missing rubber feet on stands.
- Check that the stands can be raised and lowered smoothly.
- Make sure crash cymbal straps are not overly worn and are securely tied.

(See also Box 6.3a, *Suspended Cymbals and Related Equipment,* page 175, and Box 6.3b, *Crash Cymbals and Related Equipment,* page 178)

Tambourines

- Tambourine heads should be tight. If there are tension rods, make sure they are evenly tuned.
- Check for missing tension rods.

(See also Box 6.4a, *Recommended Tambourines,* page 183)

Triangles, Beaters, and Clamps

- Make sure that you have proper clamps for your triangles, and that the string holding the triangle is in good condition.
- Make sure that the clamp has an extra safety string.
- Check that you have good, metal beaters.

(See also Box 6.5a, *Triangles and Related Equipment,* page 187)

Wood Blocks

- Check for cracks.
- If you are investing in new wood blocks, you might like "jam blocks" which are made of plastic. They sound very good and will last.

Percussion Table

- If your budget allows, invest in a percussion table. Be sure to have something soft on top of it (a folded towel, foam) so that instruments can be picked up and put down quickly and quietly.

INSPECTING YOUR DRUMS AND TIMPANI
Drumheads

- Check all your drum and timpani heads. To sound as best they can, the heads—both top and bottom—must be free of dents and holes, and tuned properly.

(See also Chapter 8.2, *Replacing and Tuning Drumheads*)

Snare Drum and Stand

- Check that the snare throw-off works smoothly.
- Inspect the snares. When engaged, the snare strands should be evenly tensioned and sitting snugly against the bottom head, with none bent out of shape. When you disengage the snares, they should drop fully away from the head so that they remain silent even when the drum is played loudly. The snare tension is adjusted with the snare adjustment knob. Make sure the snares are tight enough to get a good snap out of the drum without choking the sound.
- Check that none of the tension rods are missing.
- Check for missing rubber feet on the snare stand.
- Check that the snare stand's basket opens and closes properly.
- Check that the stand can be raised and lowered smoothly.

Be sure you have snare stands that suit your needs. For concert playing, you need stands that can be lifted high enough for a student when

standing. Drum sets need stands that can go quite low. Some stands have a range of height suitable for both concert and set playing.
(See also Box 2.1a, *Snare Drum and Related Equipment,* page 18)

Tom toms

• Check for missing tension rods.

See "Drumheads" above.

Timpani

• Check that the timpani heads are clear (in tune with themselves), and that the drums can play through the required range of notes.
• Make sure you have timpani covers—and that they are used.

See "Drumheads" above
(See also Box 5.1a, *Timpani and Related Equipment,* page 154)

Mallet instruments

With each of your mallet instruments, check that:

• the frame is solid and that all screws are in place and tightened
• the bar cord and springs (on the vibraphone, marimba and xylophone) are in good shape and the cord is taut
• the bars are in tune. (If there is a problem, there's not much you can do short of sending the bars to a tuner or buying a new instrument.)
On the vibraphone:
• Check the foot pedal. When the pedal is up, none of the bars should sustain when hit. When it is down, all the bars should be clear of the felt and ring freely. If there is a problem, try adjusting the spring, situated under the bars, which regulates the tension of the dampening mechanism.
On the glockenspiel:
• Check that the bar mounting screws and rubber bushings, that keep the bars in position on the frame, are secure and in good condition.

(See also Box 4.1a, *Mallet Instruments and Related Equipment,* page 126)

Taking Stock of Your Mallets

It is extremely important that you have the right mallet(s) available for each instrument. Playing a bass drum with a timpani mallet will not do. And you won't produce the cymbal roll you're looking for using mallets that are too hard.

You'll need a selection of mallets that includes:

Bass Drum Mallets

• A good quality mallet, with substantial weight and a dense felt.
• A matched pair of bass drum mallets for playing rhythmic passages and rolls.

Timpani Mallets

Ideally, three pair of mallets are needed:

• a general purpose pair
• a pair with larger, softer heads when less attack is desired
• a hard pair for staccato passages and for greater definition when playing high notes and quieter passages.

Note: The felt on bass drum and timpani mallets can easily become worn and frayed. Students should avoid handling the felt directly, and mallets should be stored in their original plastic covers. If strands of felt separate from the head – often taking the form of hanging, fluffy balls – the heads should be trimmed with a scissors. Once the layer of felt becomes too thin, it must be replaced.

Xylophone Mallets:

• Several pair of mallets made of hard rubber, plastic, and tightly woven yarn over a hard core. Mallets with rattan handles, rather than plastic, are better quality.

(See also Box 4.1a, *Mallet Instruments and Related Equipment,* page 126)

Vibraphone and Marimba Mallets:

- Several pair of mallets appropriate to each instrument.
- Double sets of mallets needed to play 4-mallet parts.

(See also Box 4.1a, *Mallet Instruments and Related Equipment,* page 126)

Cymbal Mallets:

- Pairs of yarn mallets, medium hard and medium soft, depending on the desired attack.

Percussion Inventory and Repair Checklist

The following Checklist is provided to help teachers take stock of percussion equipment, and note what repairs or purchases are required.

Instruments and mallets/sticks are listed in bold, followed by a list of parts and accessories to be inspected, mallet recommendations and, if applicable, a reminder to check tuning. For further information regarding instrument and mallet care, see Chapter 8.3, *An Overview of Percussion Inventory and Instrument Maintenance*.

Instrument/Mallets component parts/accessories	Repair	Purchase
Snare Drum head, tension rods, snares, throw-off		
Snare Drumsticks drum set, concert models		
Tom-Toms heads, tension rods		
Bass Drum head, stand		
Bass Drum Beaters pair, single general		

Suspended Cymbals stands, felts, sleeves, cup washers, mallets		
Crash Cymbals straps		

Timpani   1 (high)
              2
              3
              4 (low)
heads, tuning gauges, pedals		

Timpani Mallets general, soft, hard		
Xylophone bar cords, frame repair, tuning		
Xylophone Mallets plastic, rubber (yarn)		
Marimba bar cords, frame repair, tuning		
Marimba Mallets (double set for four mallet parts)		
Vibraphone bar cords, frame repair, tuning		
Vibraphone Mallets (double set for four mallet parts)		
Glockenspiel bar cords, frame repair, tuning		
Glockenspiel Mallets plastic		
Wood Blocks stand		

Wood Block Mallets suitable plastic or other hard mallet		
Triangle beaters, clamps		
Tambourine head, lugs		
Guiro		
Maracas		
Castanets		
Sleigh Bells		
Whistles		
Horns		

Book Recommendations

The following list of recommended books is by no means comprehensive. The number of good books available is enormous, and growing all the time. Aside from a few recommendations, those included here are books that I have used in my own teaching studio over the years and enjoyed playing from.

They are designated as beginning, intermediate, or advanced-level material—which should be used as rough guidelines. I've listed a beginning book as one suitable for a student just starting to read music who has little or no previous experience playing percussion. That being our guideline, the books on Latin drumming, for example, fall into the intermediate category due to the reading and coordination skills required, even though a specific book may be considered a beginning-level Latin drum set method.

I encourage you to briefly familiarize yourself with a book before purchasing to confirm that it is suitable for your students' needs.

SNARE TECHNIQUE

Alfred's Drum Method: Book 1 (beginning)
Dave Black and Sandy Feldstein; Alfred Music

Alfred's Drum Method: Book 2 (intermediate)
Dave Black and Sandy Feldstein; Alfred Music

Syncopation (beginning–intermediate)
Ted Reed; Alfred Music

Stick Control (intermediate–advanced)
George Lawrence Stone; George B. Stone and Son

Wrist Twisters: A Musical Approach to Snare Drumming (intermediate–advanced)
Elden C. "Buster" Bailey; Keyboard Percussion Publications

SNARE DRUM SOLOS

Alfred's Beginning Snare Drum Solos (collected solos included in *Alfred's Drum Method 1*, earlier) (beginning)
Dave Black & Sandy Feldstein; Alfred Music

Alfred's Intermediate Snare Drum Solos (collected solos included in *Alfred's Drum Method 2*, above) (intermediate)
Dave Black & Sandy Feldstein; Alfred Music

The All-American Drummer (intermediate–advanced)
Charley Wilcoxon; Ludwig Music Publishing

America's N.A.R.D. Solos (intermediate–advanced)
Various authors; Ludwig Music

Portraits in Rhythm (advanced)
Anthony Cirone; Alfred Music

Douze Études pour Caisse-Claire (advanced)
Jacques Delécluse; Alphonse Leduc

Rudimental Drum Solos for the Marching Snare Drummer (advanced)
Ben Hans; Hal Leonard

PERCUSSION SOLOS

Solos for the Percussion Player (intermediate–advanced)
John O'Reilly; Schirmer/Hal Leonard

GENERAL DRUM SET

Groove Essentials (beginning–advanced) (includes jazz, Latin, and rock styles)
Tommy Igoe; Hudson Music

JAZZ DRUMMING

Drumset Essentials (Vols. 1–3) (beginning–advanced)
Peter Erskine; Alfred Music

The Art of Bop Drumming (intermediate–advanced)
John Riley; Manhattan Music

Chart Reading Workbook for Drummers (intermediate–advanced)
Bobby Gabriele; Hal Leonard

ROCK DRUMMING

The Drumset Musician (beginning–intermediate)
Rod Morgenstein and Rick Mattingly; Hal Leonard

Ultimate Realistic Rock (beginning–intermediate)
Carmen Appice; Warner Bros. Publications

Contemporary Drumset Techniques (intermediate–advanced)
Rick Latham; Rick Latham Publishing Company

Advanced Funk Studies (intermediate–advanced)
Rick Latham; Rick Latham Publishing Company

The New Breed (advanced)
Gary Chester; Modern Drummer Publications

LATIN DRUMMING

Drum Atlas: Drum Styles from around the World (intermediate)
Various Authors; Alfred Music

Afro-Cuban Coordination for Drumset: The Essential Method and Workbook
(intermediate–advanced)
Maria Martinez; Musicians Institute Press

Brazilian Coordination for Drumset: The Essential Method and Workbook
(intermediate–advanced)
Maria Martinez; Musicians Institute Press

Afro-Cuban Rhythms for Drumset (advanced)
Frank Malabe and Bob Weiner; Manhattan Music

MALLET TECHNIQUES

Fundamental Method for Mallets (beginning–intermediate)
Mitchell Peters; Alfred Music

Mental and Manual Calisthenics for the Modern Mallet Player (intermediate–advanced)
Elden "Buster" Bailey; Henry Adler

Modern School for Xylophone, Marimba, Vibraphone (intermediate–advanced)
Morris Goldenberg; Alfred Music

Four-Mallet Marimba Playing: A Musical Approach for All Levels (intermediate–advanced)
Nancy Zeltsman; Hal Leonard

Vibraphone Technique: Dampening and Pedaling (intermediate–advanced)
(for four-mallet playing; presents techniques through the study of solo pieces)
David Friedman; Steve Weiss Music

MALLET SOLOS

Fundamental Studies for Mallets (beginning)
Garwood Whaley; J.R. Publications

Mirror from Another: A Collection of Solo Pieces for Vibraphone (intermediate–advanced)
David Friedman; Alfred Music

Masterpieces for Marimba (intermediate–advanced)
Arr. Thomas MacMillan; Alfred Music

The Jazz Vibraphone Book: Etudes in the Style of the Masters (intermediate–advanced)
Dick Sisto; Meredith Music

Best of Bach: 12 Solo Arrangements with CD Accompaniment (intermediate)
(Note: This book is for violin.)
Arr. by Donald Sosin; Cherry Lane Music Company

TIMPANI TECHNIQUES

Fundamental Method for Timpani (beginning–intermediate)
Mitchell Peters; Alfred Music

Modern Method for Timpani (beginning–intermediate)
Saul Goodman; Alfred Music

The Solo Timpanist (advanced)
Vic Firth; Carl Fischer

INDEX

Page numbers in italics indicate illustrations.

Made in the USA
Columbia, SC
22 July 2019